Zen and the Art of Sales
An Eastern Approach to Western Commerce

Blake Messer

Copyright © 2012 Blake Messer

All rights reserved.

ISBN-13: 978-1481053235

DEDICATION

For Max.

Great Start [illegible]
For the Beginning —
Go... Quite . . .

"However many holy words you read,
however many you speak,
what good will they do you
if you do not act on upon them?"

Buddha

This is the answer! —
To Make a New Order
In Life — Someone Will
Grow!

CONTENTS

	Acknowledgments	i
1	The Western Notion of Selling	1
2	Finding Purpose in Sales	5
3	Finding Prosperity	9
4	Meditation	11
5	Goal Setting	14
6	Karma Leads to Commerce	18
7	Hard to Say No	21
8	Managing Maybe	24
9	All Parties Present	28
10	Making Action Happen Faster	32
11	Ask for the Order	35
12	Detaching from the Result	38
13	Karmic Negotiation – Pricing Strategy	40

14	The Pitch	45
15	The Bruce Lee Close	50
16	Addressing Objections	54
17	Work Rate – Excuses	58
18	Evoke Emotion	62
19	It's All About Them	66
20	Mantra Advertising	73
21	The Leak & Impermanence	79
22	Frequency not Frequently	81
23	Good Ads Can't Change a Bad Business	86
24	Collections and Avoiding Attrition	89
25	Your Journey	96

ACKNOWLEDGMENTS

A special thanks to my best friend, David Brauhn, who edited this humble book. David also designed the cover and has honored me with his friendship for many years.

Thanks to: Brandi Messer, Rob Skinner, Joan Messer, Laurie & Jamie Merkel, Dr. Dan Etulain, Ryan Hoerner, Cub Scout Pack 955, Doc Holliday, Steve Rhyner, Quentin Whiting, Ken Fearnow, The Ketchikan Chamber of Commerce, Martin & Lorine Messer, Carol Rucker, Peter Fletcher, Scott Schramm, Scotty Campbell, Marco Hernandez, my clients and their staffs, The Residents of Sitka, America's Broadcasters, The Stronger Business Initiative Chamber of Commerce Sponsors and Attendees, and America's entrepreneurs.

zen |zen|
noun
ORIGIN, Japanese, literally *meditation*. A technique used to know oneself and to manifest an accurate nature of life; unfolding from moment to moment without biases.

art |ärt|
noun
The expression or application of human creative skill and imagination, producing works to be appreciated primarily for their beauty or emotional power.

sales |sāls|
noun
The exchange of a commodity or service for money within an expressed period of time.

CHAPTER 1
THE WESTERN
NOTION OF SELLING

My first sale made me feel triumphant! I sensed that I had moved the needle of progress forward, helped myself, and helped the enterprise that I was representing. And I knew I would help my newly acquired client succeed.

Years whirled past, I kept climbing the ladder of success, and I found myself on a professional journey to learn the craft of sales. I devoured any published knowledge on the matter I came across. I became a student of psychology and human desire. I even sought out and indentured myself to those I saw as "masters of the craft."

My drive and know-how took me far in sales. I felt I could effectively sell whatever to whomever. I wound up being in demand as a sales trainer, parroting all of the techniques I had learned. I was good at that, too. My charisma and desire to help people allowed me to assist many sales people and entrepreneurs, along with my own company's sales efforts.

Over the years, I took part in more than 18,000 sales negotiations. Some negotiations were fruitful, and some were not. This wealth of experience helped me realize a new level of understanding of my profession.

However, my responsibilities and tensions grew along with my prosperity. By anyone's measure, I was successful at sales, but still I would have negotiations that failed. Why did they fail? I was successful at teaching my methods, but despite my efforts, I was still unable to affect lasting change in the lives of trainees as I had hoped. How could I help them in a more meaningful way?

My anxiety began to grow. If I failed to produce a sale, I wore that failure like an albatross from my neck. I could see others did, too. I saw many dedicated people abandon their burgeoning careers. Others hid amid the shadows of mediocrity.

Anxiety turned into despair, and despair to agony. I was physically in pain. The more I failed, the harder I worked and the more I focused. I tried to control all of the factors, but I found that made me even less successful. All that I had learned told me that the difference between desperation and prosperity was determined by how hard I worked, so I worked harder. This led to a very difficult time in my life. I blamed others and found pointless excuses to justify my situation. My formerly sunny disposition was replaced with a bleak outlook.

I looked back at the people who taught me how to sell and at the people I taught how to sell, and I saw many of them were afflicted with the same problems that haunted me. .

I needed to find new teachers.

If you're reading this, there is a strong chance that you have found yourself in a career, position, or path that requires you to sell a product or a service, and you are uneasy about the process.

The first question you should ask yourself is, "Why am I uncomfortable with having to sell"?

Is it the possibility of rejection you fear? Is it the fear of seeming to be manipulative and the stigma associated with "sales" you don't like?

Do you fear failure? An old Japanese proverb says, "Fear is only as deep as one's mind allows." These fears are manifested only inside of ourselves. Letting these fears control or influence your life hampers commerce and limits abundance.

Western culture has aligned the exchange of a commodity or service for money in an expressed period of time with shame. This arbitrary alignment has been one of the most limiting forces in our culture today.

Without sales and the people who make those transactions happen, little would be accomplished, and civilization as we know it would not exist. Eastern cultures have developed a pragmatic, logical approach to life that can be adapted to a modern method of western commerce. This method can ultimately alleviate all of the previously mentioned fears and create serenity in your businesses and serenity in your life. This book's aim is to use this practical approach toward life and apply it to macro and micro transactional sales and negotiations that are encountered in the West.

Many lawyers work very hard in college, then even harder in law school to get a degree, pass the bar and hang a shingle for their new firm, only to find that they have inherited a "sales position." They now have to sell their services to a community that resides in a very competitive landscape. And though they have accumulated considerable courtroom skills, litigious acumen, and other legal knowledge, they lack the tools to effectively sell those services to prospective clients who certainly could benefit from what they have to offer.

Some dentists, optometrists, and medical professionals relentlessly work to gain a position at a practice or build their own only to find that, though they have become very proficient, they are now tasked with having to sell their services to potential patients. Though the medical schools of the West produce the finest professionals on the planet, few work to prepare those professionals for the most important battle – selling their services.

If you are responsible in any way for driving revenue for your business, you should understand that you are a sales person. Yet many business professionals grapple with the notion of being a sales person because of predisposed stigmas. Many allow that stigma to congest the wheels of commerce. Some hide behind busy work, blame the economy, or hire others to attempt to yield something that only they can sow.

Over 2,500 years ago, Buddha said, "The mind is everything. What we think is what we become. He is able who thinks he is able." Fast-forward through time to the early 20th century, when American business magnate Henry Ford said, "Whether you think that you can or that you can't, you are usually right." It's remarkable that these two very different people, from different cultures separated by thousands of miles and thousands of years could come to the same truthful conclusion.

These pages are filled with practical notions from some of the best thinkers who have ever lived. Some of these pages offer content about how to logically execute any sale. But more than anything, you'll discover how to find and overcome the internal obstacles that limit your own peace and abundance. In the words of Khalil Gibran, "Say not, 'I have found the truth,' but rather, 'I have found a truth.'" Here is a truth I have found.

CHAPTER 2
FINDING PURPOSE
IN SALES

Now that you've found yourself in a sales role, an appropriate question to ask yourself would be, "Why am I selling?" Really probe introspectively for the answer to this question. Are your motives strictly to put money in your bank account? Do you want to make a better life for you and your family? Is this a temporary role you intend to play until you can find what you're truly in search of?

If you've answered "Yes" to any of the above questions, then it's time to examine some hypothetical scenarios.

For the first scenario let's say you find yourself in a sales position that offers an extremely generous rate of compensation. It has a product that is easy to sell to your customer base. This hypothetical position allows you to rapidly fill your bank account, live a better life and help your family in the process. The downside is this product leads to great suffering, the deaths of many people, and irreparable harm to the Earth.

Would you still sell that product?

Another scenario to consider, what if you accept a sales role that is financially rewarding, requires little effort, but the products, or services you offer don't work?

Would you still sell that service or product?

A typical sales position requires approximately 50 hours a week in time spent on the job. This doesn't include an average commute time of 6 hours a week. Or the average preparation time of four hours every week applying make-up, tying ties, shining shoes, and performing other pedestrian tasks associated with going to work. Now let's add the time when we are not on the job yet we think about work. Is it 30 minutes a day? Is it more?

In total, there are 168 hours in a week. About 56 hours are spent sleeping, leaving 112 conscious hours. If you are in a sales role with an allocation of time described above, you're spending 64 of your conscious hours on the job every week, so roughly half of your waking life.

Now let's say you're in a sales role that reflects the first scenario described. Would you feel comfortable knowing that half of your life was spent causing suffering, death, and harm to the Earth?

To the second scenario: If you knowingly sell a product or service that doesn't do what you claim it will do, I think you would agree that is a lie. If you take money from someone under false pretenses, that is, in it's core essence, stealing. With the knowledge that half of your waking life will be rolled into your sales position, are you okay spending half of your life lying and stealing?

Most ethical people would say "No" to undertaking both of those hypothetical endeavors, but many people in sales tolerate and precipitate less egregious sales scenarios. Perhaps the product you're selling doesn't do everything the enterprise you're representing asks you to claim. Or the products lead to some degree of undue suffering to someone, somewhere.

If you are not completely comfortable with the products or services you're selling to others, you should closely examine your present sales position and then make a determination if you should carry on.

Buddha once said, "Your purpose in life is to find your purpose and give your whole heart and soul to it." Whatever we are selling needs to firmly align with whatever you have identified as your purpose; as it will consume a portion of your heart and soul. Anything that doesn't dovetail nicely with that purpose, even for a short time, could harm you and others on a very profound level.

What would you be doing if money was not an issue?

What if you had so much that you and those closest to you need never work again? Would you enjoy an endless vacation? Would you travel the world? Would you buy anything your heart desired? Would you spend yourself and your wealth in the service of others? Many of us hold the notion of service in our hearts, but we wait for the day to come when our personal needs have been met. Why are we waiting? Respected yoga guru Bikram Choudhury once said, "If you can, you must, and if you can't, you must try."

When asked the question, "Why are you here on Earth?" most moral people will respond with a variation on the same answer – "to help others." Most spiritual leaders would agree that "to help others" is an answer that deeply aligns with most of their spiritual philosophies. In fact, the Dali Lama once said, "Our prime purpose in life is to help others, and if we can't help them, at least don't hurt them."

If you feel that your purpose in life is to help others, your role in whatever you are selling also must help others. We are all born with distinct gifts. Those who haven't identified their own gifts often struggle to fulfill their purpose. The best of humanity finds ways to utilize their unique gifts to help meet their needs and fulfill their purpose of helping others.

Almost regardless of what we sell, whether it is concrete girders or advertising that will be over in 30 seconds, everything is impermanent. At some point, that product or service will be no more. What remains are our actions, if those actions are executed in the spirit of helping others, we will find wealth by giving. Not just the giving of our product or service at an honorable price, but also the giving of our time, our presence, our focus, and our commitment to whatever it is we have sold.

CHAPTER 3
FINDING PROSPERITY

Prosperity in sales is often associated with great effort. And many think this prosperity comes at the expense of others. Many people have met their sales quotas time and time again by exerting, relentlessly haggling and routinely experience strife in the process, but are they truly prosperous? If you experience anxieties, drama, fear, and contentions are on your path to achieving your sales goal, you are more impoverished than if you did nothing and did not receive a paycheck.

Money is only a single element of true prosperity in sales. Prosperity includes liberty, creativity, balance, strong bonds with co-workers and customers, and physical and emotional health.

Prosperity in sales could be defined as the ongoing proliferation of abundance for others and ourselves. True prosperity is the ability to fulfill your goals with the least effort possible.

Often times it is ourselves or others who set limits on goals and attempt to define what can be achieved in the realm of prosperity. When we understand that we are in charge of our own success and the limitations we perceive are simply an illusion, we can achieve anything our hearts desire. Our internal position is the thing that commands what we can accomplish, not experiences, circumstances, or arbitrary expectations defined by others.

If we are seeking prosperity by attempting to please supervisors or clients, then we anticipate receiving praise for our actions. We hope for the carrot and fear the stick.

If we hinge our happiness or peace on the reaction of our supervisors or clients, we are turning over our potential prosperity and serenity over to them and in turn applying meaningless limits on our own success.

The same can be said by limiting our happiness to a perfect sales circumstance. If we work to control every component of every sale it will only lead to disappointment and ultimately suffering. No matter how much we prepare, there will never be a perfect sales circumstance.

The need for approval and the need to control things can both be rendered down to the same limiting force: fear.

Imagine if you could shed the shackles of fear, if you could be fearless in the face of any challenge, if you were invulnerable to judgment of others, and if you could feel equal to anyone who has ever lived past or present. If you could achieve that bold nature, any perceived limitation would be meaningless.

To become fearless, we must first find clarity. Clarity is not found in a place or bestowed from another; rather, clarity is found inside one's self. Since prehistoric times, Eastern cultures have been introspectively meditating to cast off the tethers of fear, achieve clarity, and embrace the potential of limitless possibilities.

CHAPTER 4
MEDITATION

Many Westerners are apprehensive about engaging in meditation, but this critical practice helps one to find introspective peace, increase creativity, aid in focus, and reduce fear and anxiety. It has been known to offer countless physical benefits including lowering blood pressure.

Meditation can be done for as little as 10 to 15 minutes daily and should be conducted in a comfortable silent place where no one will interrupt you in the time you intend to meditate. Lie down, or sit in a comfortable chair with both feet on the ground, palms face down on your legs, eyes shut and your back straight.

Begin by breathing in as deep as you can and hold your breath for six long counts. Then exhale slowly for six long counts. Once your lungs have been completely expelled for six long counts, inhale deeply and slowly for six long counts. Continue that process four times with your mind focused on nothing but the process of breathing.

When you've completed five full breath cycles, begin to breath normally and focus on your body. Imagine every body part relaxing, starting with your toes and slowly working your way up to the crown of your head. If you loose your focus or if random thoughts wander into your head, acknowledge them, but usher them out quickly by returning your focus to your body and your breath.

Upon concluding a relaxing scan of your body, focus for 30 seconds on something or someone in your life that you're grateful for. Savor that gratitude, as it a critical catalyst in helping you find a strong meditative state that will aid you in achieving limitless possibilities.

To gain clarity, we must be in command of our thoughts. Commanding our thoughts is much like trying to control your heart rate. You can't tell your heart to instantly slow down to 45 beats per minute. You can, however, manage your breath and find a relaxed setting that will allow you to influence your heart rate. Your thoughts are exactly the same. If I say to you, "Elvis Presley," there is a strong chance you are picturing The King. In fact, you likely couldn't command your brain not to think about that image. Your mind cycles through thousands of thoughts every hour. When it comes to commanding our thoughts, the best we can hope to do is to influence them by focusing on our emotions.

When we lean on the emotion of gratitude, it takes our mind's focus off of itself and away from the ego and it focuses it on others or other things and how we feel them. This allows you to quickly influence your thoughts and in turn summon clarity needed for meditation.

After 30 seconds, begin saying in your head a simple four-word mantra aimed at reducing fear and opening you up to limitless possibilities. Say these four words slowly, "abundance, health, clarity, kindness." Repeat them for as long as you need to find a peaceful meditative state. When you say the words, work to feel their deeper meaning. When you say "abundance" imagine an abundant life for your self and those around you. Imagine abundance for those who make the products you're selling, envision abundance for those who buy your product or service and imagine the abundance propelled by them to others. When you say the word "health," imagine a fit and healthy body for you and other whose lives you have and will impact. When saying "clarity" to yourself, visualize yourself speaking and understanding things with laser focus and a limber mind. When you say "kindness" to yourself, imagine yourself helping others with your generosity, compassion, and understanding.

Meditation takes practice; so don't get discouraged if you fail to achieve a modicum of peace or clarity in your first couple attempts. The word "yoga" has been translated to mean "union," meaning the union of body and mind, or "moving meditation." As they've said in countless yoga classes over the centuries, "Trying produces the same benefit as doing." That is certainly true with meditation.

CHAPTER 5
GOAL SETTING

The standard method for setting goals has been assessing how much revenue is required then assigning a goal amount that you are expected to achieve within a frame of time. Usually that number is overestimated slightly to allow for shortcomings in performance. Oftentimes, the established frame of time comes and goes and that revenue goal is not met. Following that goal failure, blame and questions usually fly about what went wrong. Many times, the person assigning the revenue amount is pinning his or her hopes on what you will produce for them. Or, if we are the ones assigning the revenue amount, we tend to pin our hopes on what our clients or customers will or won't do. Either way this approach is short sighted and flawed at many levels, primarily because it's based in fear and the desire to control the outcome. Both of those flawed methods will only lead to disappointment and suffering.

There is another tack in setting and achieving sales goals. It is as follows.

1. Wish it.
2. Set your intent.
3. Visualize.

Let's start with "Wish it." It may seem trivial or childish to wish. If you do nothing more than make a wish without taking subsequent actions needed to manifest intent, nothing will happen. However, anything that has ever come to be is a result of a person's actions that have blossomed from a wish.

Wishing alone for a goal to be fulfilled most often will lead to disappointment. This is why after a goal has been set and a wish to fulfill that goal has been made, intense awareness of that wish is required.

The next critical step in achieving goals is to set your intent. Intent is the motivating force of any wish. Intent is a wish without the desire to control the outcome. In the Hawaiian spiritual tradition of Huna, one of the principal beliefs is "energy flows where attention goes." A core law of physics states "energy can ever be destroyed; it can only be transferred." Focusing your attention on a wish can begin the transfer of your own energy toward manifesting your intent in reality. Think about when you smell food cooking when you're somewhat hungry. Your awareness is focused for a moment on that smell. Your senses and slight wish to eat are aroused and there is a strong chance that your intent to eat will manifest in you finding something to put in your stomach.

If the Huna principal is correct, and if we put our attention on any shortfall of our goal, we will likely devote energy to the shortfall, rather than to the fulfilling intent to achieve that goal. The steps on the path to taking your intent to realizing your goal will undoubtedly be wrought with difficulty. If we can create a way for these difficulties to offer a solution to achieve our goal and focus our awareness on that opportunity, energy will flow in the direction of the opportunity.

Intent coupled with awareness allows more energy to flow to manifesting a goal. Nature has boundless ways of orchestrating events when energy is applied. The universe features countless suns that hold, heat, and power infinite numbers of planets. Energy conducts these complex, efficient symphonies. Nature figures out how to put that energy into the perfect motion. Similarly, do not concern yourself with the actions in the goal setting process. Just apply energy.

Meditation upon specific goals, wishes, and intent helps to focus your determination and drive energy and awareness. To that end, meditation will help you realize any goal you desire to achieve. When meditating on your goals, visualize yourself reaching those goals and imagine what it would feel like to accomplish your goals. Relish that feeling; not just the thought of manifesting your goal. If the shallowest doubt begins to infiltrate your thoughts, recognize the fact that you're having those thoughts, and then shepherd them out of your mind as quickly as they crept in by imagining the feelings you'll have when you reach your goal. The visualization of reaching your goals in a meditative state is critical, because it helps make the blueprint for the course of action.

This may seem insignificant, but it's similar to driving for the first time in a strange city. If you've ever been plunged into a situation where you're behind the wheel in an unfamiliar metropolis without the aid of GPS navigation, you'll agree that traveling can be rough. You might miss exits, or go down one-way streets, or hear a barrage of horns from local motorists who have no patience for someone learning the ropes of their local roads. Typically, this is a stressful process wrought with anxiety, hesitation, and trepidation that leads to more risk while you're traveling these new freeways. Though you may make it to your destination in one piece, you'll likely be late, and the experience can be nerve rattling.

Now, let's say you have a week to travel the roads of that new city. Repetition and experience allows you to recall the proper routes, and travel gets easier. You begin to look for landmarks that indicate where your next turn resides; you calm down and get to your destination with much more ease. Visualizing the broad strokes of accomplishing your goal serves the same function as traveling down the same road more than once. Do not focus on the minor details or the precise actions, as that is a service of Karma and the role of the sale, which we will uncover next. Instead, focus more on what realizing your goal will mean. If your goal is to have more money, then visualize more money in your bank account. If your goal is to achieve a difficult task, then in your mind revel in that feeling of accomplishment. Buddha once said, "All we are is the result of what we thought."

CHAPTER 6
KARMA LEADS TO COMMERCE

The Sanskrit word "Karma" is broadly defined by Hinduism, Buddhism, and Jainism as the force generated by a person's actions and the ethical consequences of those actions, which determine the nature of the person's next existence.

Not only do these faiths and philosophies hold that your present and past actions impact your immediate future, but they also hold that those actions impact the future of your next life. Many Westerners grapple with the notion of reincarnation. Wherever your personal philosophies fall on the matter, certainly you can identify with the notion of "cause and effect," "we reap what we sow," or "you get what you give."

If we look to the dynamics of the physical world, Newton's third law corroborates Karma: "For every action there is an equal and opposite reaction." This law can be represented by what happens when one boat moves at a rate of three knots on a lake. If that moving boat then bumps into a boat sitting completely still, then the boat that was sitting still will be put into motion. Karma in sales works precisely the same way. We offer a product or service, and something will result from the action of our offer. What that something is and when it manifests are hard to define, but something will happen from the action taken.

If we had to simplify the Sanskrit definition of Karma, then it would be action. Karma is action. In the context of sales, the right action is everything. Our job as salespeople is not to get people to do things or buy stuff they do not need or want. Our job as salespeople is not to persuade, cajole, or convince others to fall in line with our beliefs or desires. Our job as sales people is to make action happen faster, whether that action is getting a "no" or a "yes" from a prospective client. This is the goal of a sale.

The hardest word for one person to say to another is "no." Buyers shy away from giving sellers a candid negative answer, even if they sincerely don't need that product or service.

If you have a child and you take her to a store, then there's a good chance that the child will find candy, a toy, or something else that she wants. Most of the time, if the child's parent doesn't intend to buy what she desires, then the parent will tell the child "next time," or "I'll think about it." Most parents will not give a candid "no," and the reason is they want to sustain a measure of peace with the child and avoid the fallout of potential conflict. Most parents understand that if they can allow the child to foster a small degree of hope, then the child will not throw a fit in the store and will soon forget about the momentary desire.

Buyers in Western cultures perform a similar dance with those who are selling. Think about the last time you were at a clothing store. A store employee probably came up to you and asked, "Can I help you with anything?" Our gut reaction is to say, "I'm just looking." Under no circumstances would we ever simply say the sweet, single-syllable word "no."

Why not? What is wrong with "no"? The answer is this: Nothing is wrong with hearing "no" from a prospective buyer. Western cultures have been conditioned that telling someone "no" is in some way harming that person, so rather than being truthful, buyers will employ a "maybe".

strategy that they hope, on a subconscious level, will not make sellers feel rejection, or at a more primal level, respond with conflict. But, in reality, by not serving up a candid "no," buyers harm sellers; they cost sellers time by not allowing them to execute the primary purpose of a sale, to make action happen faster. They are putting up a Karmic roadblock. Mahatma Gandhi once said, "A 'no' uttered from the deepest conviction is better than a 'yes' merely uttered to please, or worse, to avoid trouble."

CHAPTER 7
HARD TO SAY "NO"

A couple of years ago, my seven-year-old son, Max, wanted to join the Cub Scouts. After a year of whittling, gluing popsicle sticks to things, and sewing on badges, it was time to sell pre-packaged popcorn to raise money for activities and service opportunities in our community.

A sign-up sheet was passed around to all of the dads, who picked a seven hour period during which they would stand with their sons at the entrance of a grocery store and attempt to sell popcorn to shoppers.

On our day, Max and I set up a table to display the popcorn, and I tucked in his shirt and combed down his cowlick, and we begin our task. We saw our first sales prospect approaching the store. He calmly entered the store's entrance area, spotted us and smiled. Max promptly asked the closing question, "Would you like to buy some popcorn?" The kind, smiling gentleman said, "I'll buy some on the way out." I thought to myself, "That's plausible." If I were going grocery shopping, I wouldn't want to start out my shopping expedition with a cumbersome box of something that I've already paid for, plus he'd have to explain to the clerk at check out, "This isn't popcorn from your store – it's from the Cub Scout in the entry way." As soon as the man passed, I told Max "good job," and we looked forward to the pending popcorn sale. Just then, three more people came through, each offering a smiling explanation about how they were going to buy some, but just not at this time. One lady said, "I don't have cash on me, but I'll get some in the store." While she was explaining that it her answer wasn't "no," other shoppers slipped briskly by, trying not to make eye contact with me or Max. It quickly dawned on me what was happening. The grocery store sold popcorn as good as or better than ours. Also, the popcorn we were selling was very expensive, and without the ability to take debit or credit cards, we would struggle to be as convenient as the very store people were venturing into. In addition, we happened to be parked at a store in a very liberal and progressive neighborhood in Seattle, Wash. Shortly before the attempted day of selling, the Boy Scouts of America were fighting accusation that they discriminated against parents of scouts who identified as being gay. The theories as to why people wouldn't buy our popcorn piled up in my head. But the different ways they declined our offer without saying a simple "no" piled up even faster.

It was at that time that I noticed some of the people who told us they would buy the popcorn on the way out were leaving from the other entrance of the store many yards away from were we were stationed and even farther away from where they had parked. It was clear that they didn't want to buy the popcorn, but they didn't want to have to reject my cute son. I then decided to track people's responses (I had plenty of time, because we were not selling too much popcorn.)

On average, Max asked the closing question "would you like to buy popcorn?" to about 35 people per hour. We averaged two sales per hour, (whether they actually wanted the popcorn, I don't know, but they didn't have the courage to tell us "no," nevertheless.) Of the remaining 33 possible sales, we would go on to see an average 25 people per hour evade us by giving us a bogus excuse, such as, "I'll buy on the way out," "I don't have cash," or "I just bought popcorn at the office." About 8 people per hour pretended as if they didn't hear Max and rushed into the store without making eye contact.

Why was it so difficult for these people to say "no"?

Here's a theory. Let's go way back. As communal living came to be, people evolved to be inherently amiable. As a member of a community, our ancestors knew that if conflict arose, it was best to make peace rather than war inside that community. Though a simple buying question is far from war, the same fight-or-flight response is triggered in a prehistoric portion of our brains, and most people who don't want to engage will flee or outright lie.

This avoidance of the word "no" happens in every form of sales. Unfortunately, evading the truth is what most sellers spend a majority of their time working around. Prospective buyers feel as if they are avoiding potential conflict, or altogether avoiding the fight or flight response, and by allowing you to foster false hope, they believe they are not saddling you with the burden of a "no."

How does Karma play into this? At the beginning of this chapter we defined our role as sales people as "making action happen faster." If the action we request from the buyer is "yes," then mission accomplished – you've got that sale. If the action we request from the buyer is "no," then excellent – now you can focus your time, awareness, and energy on your next potential sale.

CHAPTER 8
MANAGING "MAYBE"

Most potential buyers who are not being honest attempt to evade you the same way we evade our children in a department store when they ask for candy or a toy. They say, "I'll think about it." Inside, they are hoping that you, the sales person, will be hopeful instead of disappointed, and that you will forget about them and the fruitless offer to "follow up." The truth is, most sales people *will* forget about them, or they will foster futile hope that the client will, one day, burst through the door and say, "Yes, I *did* think about it, and I will buy this." Worse yet, sales people misinterpret that "maybe" as a "no," allowing sales people to also avoid the fight response that they are also wired with. The truth is, the client decided it was "no" on the spot but lacked the courage to be candid with the seller. The seller lacked the courage to press the prospective for a "no".

Most of the best sellers around are not the best because they hear "yes" more often than others, or because they pack their prospect pipeline full. Professional purveyors are superior sellers because they have learned how to emboldened prospective buyers into being honest, and by managing "maybe."

Karma essentially means action, and when it comes to managing "maybe," the first appropriate action we can command occurs at the point when a client says "maybe" or "I need time to think about it." When prospective buyers say, "I need time to think about it," they are responding with a gut response that neither engages the fight response nor obligates them to do something they may not want to do. Professional sellers can be prepared with the same kind of canned gut response, but one that instead puts the Karma of a sale in motion.

When the prospective buyer replies, "I need time to think about it," reply with, "So I don't waste any more of my time or your time, what precisely do you need to think about?" You'll find that there is a great likelihood your prospective buyer will come clean, right then and there, and say, "I'm really not interested in this." Eureka! The prospective buyer has just saved you the time you would have wasted conducting fruitless follow-ups calls and given you time you can now spend helping others who really do want your products or services.

Now, at this point, if the prospective buyer is someone with whom you really want to do business, you should press forward with the next step of commerce karma: Ask, "Why don't you want to buy it?" If the buyer cites a sound, rational reason, then accept "no," be kind and courteous, and move your awareness to your next opportunity. If the prospective buyer remains evasive, then you might try to inspire courage within him or her to say "no" by using another response, such as "Time is money, so if you tell me 'no,' then you'll be helping us both." Again, there is nothing wrong with "no;" it allows us to more quickly advance sales Karma.

Occasionally, a prospective buyer will declare, "I need to talk it over with my business partner (or wife, or accountant.)" Oftentimes, this is a ruse used to evade the seller. If the prospective buyer does sincerely need more time to think about your offer or to check with someone else involved in the decision-making process, grant it to him or her, but never leave a potential sale open ended. When the prospective buyer responds with "Maybe, but I need time to think about it," and after you've answered any concern that might hold up a "yes" or "no," then right there, on the spot, give the shortest amount of time possible for him or her to think about it your offer.

It shouldn't take long for prospective buyers to get input on your offer.

If prospective buyers say they need to check with someone before making a decision, and sellers say they will check back with them later, there is really no commitment from either party to advance the negotiation. It is a case where two timid creatures are fleeing from fear and wasting each other's time.

For a moment, imagine the car of your dreams. Let's say you find that car in the color you like, and the car is being sold by an individual on a corner parking lot at a busy downtown intersection. The car has a "For Sale" sign that features a phone number and a price that is about one quarter of what the car is really worth. Now, imagine that you and your significant other happen to have that amount (and more) in expendable funds in your checking account. Let's presume that you have a rule in your relationship: Big purchase decisions will always be made together, so even though it is an unbelievable deal, you still need to get your partner's blessing. To make sure the car wouldn't be purchased by someone else, you'd probably immediately talk to your partner, so that you could acquire the car of your dreams at a bargain price before someone else takes your opportunity.

Likewise, if prospective buyers are indeed interested in your product or service, then they will do whatever is necessary to quickly consult with anyone else who must be involved in the decision. Most often, potential buyers use the "I-need-to-check-with-someone" excuse as a smoke screen in a negotiation in the hopes that they can evade you

A key problem that we, as sellers, face in regards to that obstacle is this: How do we identify who is genuinely interested in buying our products or services, who truly needs more time, and who is not telling us the truth? This is where Karma, or action, comes in to play. When dealing with "maybe" in a sales negotiation, the only thing we, as sellers, can do – outside of taking the addressing their objections and then asking directly for the sale once more – is to *manage "maybe."*.

CHAPTER 9
ALL PARTIES PRESENT

When prospective buyers tell you they need more time before they can give you a definitive "yes" or "no," the action – or Karma – you need to set in motion is to negotiate a definitive time for them to give you their decision. Understand that if they are reluctant to give a specific time, then they it is likely they don't want what you are selling, or they simply lack the courage to give you a straight answer.

Here is another way we can command Karma in a "maybe" situation. When prospective buyers say, "I need to check with my business partner," ask them, "If you had to make the decision all by yourself, would you buy it?" If they say "no," the chances of the sale manifesting are slim-to-none. Think about it – are they really likely to go back to their business partners and say, "There's this person who came by to sell this thing. I don't really want it, but as your business partner, we look at all opportunities together. Here are all of the points the sales person made in the presentation, would you like to buy it?" Even if the other business partner would say "yes," 50 percent of the those with voting interests still don't want it. The sale is dead on arrival.

The best way to compel Karma in a situation where you have two parties making a decision is to have all deciding parties present for your presentation. When you're booking the appointment to give the presentation, ask specifically, "Are you the ultimate decision maker?" If they say, "No," then ask if you can set up a meeting to give your presentation to *all parties present*. Without all of them, you're spinning your wheels, and you're not really nudging the Karma of that sale along.

I learned the value of having all parties present while working in the small island community of Ketchikan Alaska. Ketchikan, a town of about 15,000, is seated in the Alexander Archipelago on the far southern panhandle of Alaska. Every year, Ketchikan sees approximately 1 million cruise ship tourists pass through as they visit the majesty that Alaska offers. Historic Ketchikan's downtown used to have an array of locally owned shops that catered to the loggers and fisherman who called Ketchikan their home.

As the quantity of tourists climbed over the years, those stores moved to areas of the community that were out of the way of the scores of stores catering to tourists. The goal of the relocated stores was to remain accessible to the townsfolk who lived there year-round.

Replacing those stores in downtown, as you can imagine, were seafood restaurants, souvenir shops, and guided tour sales booths. What you might not imagine springing up were jewelry stores. Lots of them. In fact, at one point, in a three-block area of downtown there were 44 jewelry stores! Eventually, there got to be so many jewelry stores that a committee of concerned townsfolk who were wanted to preserve the downtown's historic appeal decided to try to put an initiative on a municipal ballot that would limit or reduce the number of jewelry stores in downtown Ketchikan. For obvious reasons, this riled up the local jewelry store owners, the Chamber of Commerce, many merchants, and others who felt that trying to control the natural selection of commerce due to a whimsical notion of the past was wrong. The Chamber of Commerce asked me to help mediate this divisive issue.

After several meetings, the two parties ultimately couldn't not be brought together, so the issue went to the ballot, and Ketchikan voters decided it was wrong to inhibit viable, tax-paying businesses.

The journey had just begun for me, however. While researching this matter, I first tried to find out why there were so many jewelry stores in one little area. How can all of these stores that sell a similar product survive? What I learned galvanized my philosophies about having all parties present when trying to move the needle of Karma in a sale.

I learned that most of the people who visit Alaska on a cruise ship are retired, middle-class married couples. Most often, they have worked and saved all of their lives and have a nice nest egg in the bank, but certainly not abundant wealth by anyone's standards. People are much more open to opportunity while on vacation, but that is not enough of a justification for 44 similar stores to reside in a three-block area.

I learned from the store owners that they really didn't see a high quantity of daily sales. In fact, some saw less than one sale a day! But the profit margin in the jewelry industry was up to 1,200 percent, and the average sale (depending on the store) ranged from $500 to $30,000. It was obvious that these jewelry stores simply needed to make one or two big sales a week in order to take care of their overhead and net a tidy profit.

The proliferation of one type of store category still didn't add up completely to me. The demographics of those coming off the cruise ships certainly did not seem to match the demographics of the people who acquire $30,000 pieces of jewelry. It was at that point that I polled a circle of married male friends, "I asked them if you had an extra $30,000 in disposable income, and all of your bills were paid, would you go into a jewelry store and spend it all on a piece of jewelry?" The answer every time was "no," and, oddly, the reason was identical every time.

All married males said a variation of, "I would be afraid I would get something she didn't like." I asked the same thing of an array of married women. Obviously, most men wouldn't want an opulent piece of jewelry to wear, so the question was slightly different: "If you had an extra $30,000 in disposable income, and all of your bills were paid, would you go into a jewelry store and spend all of that money on a piece of jewelry?" Every one of them answered in exactly the same fashion: "No, I would never spend that kind of money on myself."

This is where the reason for congestion of jewelry stores in Ketchikan Alaska became obvious. I later learned from the jewelry store owners that those two distinct objections I found in my informal polls are easily overcome when both the wife and husband are together. Think about it: a retired couple has worked hard their whole lives, raised and put children through college, paid off mortgages and debts, and accrued a modest retirement income and savings. They are on vacation, and what better way for a husband to celebrate his wife than to buy her a beautiful heirloom commemorating an adventure together that she can pass down to her family? Those sales would never manifest and the Karma of those sales wouldn't transpire without all parties present.

Chances are, you're not selling jewelry to cruise ship tourists, but the lesson remains. To help affect the Karma of a sales situation that has only a portion of the decision team present, other actions will need to be taken.

CHAPTER 10
MAKING ACTION HAPPEN FASTER

So, taking what we have learned so far, let's take a look at the same scenario we've been dealing with: You approach a prospective buyer, and he or she says, "I need to check with my business partner"

You reply with, "OK, to maximize both of our schedules, I'll give you a time. Can you check with your business partner while we are both here? Perhaps we could get all parties together on a conference call right now?"

You have just attempted to take action; the wheels of Karma are in motion. At first, this may feel uncomfortable, but rest easy knowing that most professional negotiations include a term limit on any offer. If prospective buyers aren't willing to give decisions within a reasonable timeframe, then they, most likely, are not really interested. If this is the case, then plot a course to embolden prospective buyers to give you a "no." A "no" is always better than a "maybe" when it comes to sales. With "no" we can devise our next action. With a duplicitous "maybe", we have nothing but hope and fear: the hope that the sale will manifest and the fear that it doesn't.

It is very hard to pay the bills with either hope or fear.

If your prospective buyers waffle when you attempt to usher a decision or meeting with them and their counterparts sooner by saying, "No, we cannot call them right now – I'll check with them and get back to you." Explain that it's your obligation to follow up, not theirs. Go on to offer and ask for a decision by the end of the business day. If that is not possible, or they counter with, "I can give you an answer in a couple weeks," then counter by saying, "I can give you 24 hours for a decision." If they say, "That's not likely going to happen within that timeframe," then make one final gesture and offer them 48 hours to come to a decision regarding your offer. If they say "no" because of the time constraint, then understand a "no" right now or in 48 hours would be a "no" in two weeks or two months. If and when they agree to a 48-hour-or-less follow up appointment for a decision, then be sure to get them to agree to a scheduled time for that follow-up meeting or call. This is true Karma sales management.

When it comes to "maybe" we, as sales people, naturally tend to foster hope. We hold the hope of approval for a decision, but by hoping for the maybe to turn into "yes," we are relying on the actions others to dictate our happiness or suffering. True happiness can only come from ourselves and is represented by our present serenity. Rather than pinning our joy or suffering to the actions of others, focus only on the action, or Karma we can command. Managing a follow-up time on "maybe" is a pure example of this.

Understand that the more time you put between your offer and the follow-up that you grant the prospective buyer, the less apt they are to buy your product or service. If, in the above example, the prospective buyer asks for more time to make a decision, then negotiate the tentative decision sooner than the client suggests. Again our job as sales people is to make action happen *faster*.

In the example, the buyer said he or she couldn't call for a decision right now, so the seller asked for a decision by the close of business. When the buyer wanted more time, the seller gave the buyer 48 hours. I call this professional bargaining for time "Karmic Negotiation," and this tactic should be employed at every point of the sale including pricing.

Implementing Karmic Negotiation in a pricing strategy helps you and the prospective buyer come to an agreeable conclusion of your negotiation. It also allows the seller to maximize each transaction and makes you and your customer or client true partners in escorting the transaction's goals.

CHAPTER 11
ASK FOR THE ORDER

Years ago, I began consulting around 190 radio and television stations owned by large and small broadcast companies. These companies ranged from publicly traded corporations in the largest cities in America to stations in the smallest of small towns.

My core mission when contracting for these media companies was to make the sales people more efficient at delivering advertising and advertising schedules that were more potent.

When I first began working with many of these sales people, I was dumbfounded when I realized that the vast majority of them would not ask for the order on a sales call. In market after market, town after town, I encountered the same thing. I would go on calls with sales people, they would pull out a produced, pre-designed broadcast package, give it to the prospective advertisers, talk about how wonderful their stations were, then compliment the prospective advertisers by saying heir existing clients love them. Most of the time, the sales people would offer to leave before the prospective advertisers had time to brush them off by saying, "Let me think about it."

In about 65 percent of the sales calls I tracked, the sales people failed to say, "Would you like to buy this?" On the calls where the sales people did manage to ask for the prospective advertisers' business, they oftentimes would not allow their prospective advertisers to answer *at all* and without provocation would ask, "Would you like me to check back with you?"

Other times, I would hear the sales people ask for the business and then not stop talking. They literally talked themselves out of the sales.

On a couple of bright occasions, I did hear the sales people ask for the orders, shut their mouths, and respectfully wait for the prospective advertisers to respond, but if their answer was anything but "yes," most often, the sales people tucked their tails between their legs and left. It was very rare when I heard them competently address the potential advertisers' concerns or objections and even rarer still when I witnessed the sales people manage to set definitive follow-up times for a decision.

Why was this the state of affairs in that industry?

Part of the reason has to do with the kind of transaction that was taking place. Sales people in media, insurance, pharmaceuticals, or any industry that deals in transactional, local, direct sales battle precisely the same dilemma. People in those fields are responsible for filling up their prospect pipelines. They are charged with managing the sales processes, the quality control of the delivery of the products, the clients' expectations, the clients' objections, negotiations, service after the sale, and collection of payment. And, more importantly, through it all they must govern their own emotions and fears associated with possible rejection.

If we were to compare transactional, local, direct sales to the sales process that takes place at restaurants, the dynamics are entirely different. The servers (the sales people for the restaurant) are not responsible for filling up the pipeline with prospective customers. The restaurant patrons that appear come due to advertisements or other outside influences most often not motivated by the person serving the food. In restaurants, the sale, negotiation, packaging are handled by the menus; the quality control is handled by the chefs; the payments and collections are handled by the customers so graciously, that, most often they leave tips of 20 percent or more. All the servers are required to do in the way of influencing the sales is to affably and accurately record the order and possibly up-sell dessert or cocktails to their patrons. If the servers ask, "Would you like dessert?" never do they take ownership of the diners' responses. They simply take the orders or bring the checks.

Transactional, local, direct sellers are often unduly vested in the responses of their clients, because they are responsible for so many different aspects of the sales process. Transactional, local, direct sellers are frequently attached to the results, feel anxiety regarding the clients' responses, and live in a world of hope and fear dictated by the actions of others.

The Buddha once said, "Do not dwell in the past. Do not dream of the future. Concentrate the mind on the present moment." Focusing on what has been or what will be cannot help you achieve your sales goals. Determination and an unwavering belief in the action you're taking right now *can*. If you avoid focusing any of your present moment awareness on barriers, the future has a greater chance to unfold in the shape of your wishes and intent.

CHAPTER 12
DETATCHING FROM THE RESULT

If you are in a transactional, local, direct sales role, one of the parts of your job that you might grapple with is detaching from the results after you ask for an order. What prospective buyers do or do not do is out of your control; you can only command your feelings and your Karma.

In my years of coaching scores of transactional, local, direct sales people, I have encountered many different excuses for why they couldn't manifest sales. Those reasons include:

"My clients are different."
"This market is different."
"Our product is different."
"I sell differently from most people."
"They really haven't had a chance to look at my proposal."
"They are going to buy something – just not this product."
"In this economy, no one is buying anything."
"Everyone is on vacation this month."
"They would buy from me, but they hate the sales manager."
"I'm too busy with all of my other tasks."

Obviously, this is a catalog of excuses, but more to the point, all of those phrases represent sales people who blame others for their own perceived failures. The reason for this is those excuse makers haven't come to the realization that prospective buyers don't reject sales people personally; rather, prospective buyers are rejecting the specific offers at the moment they are being offered. If sales people were to accept or personally own every piece of rejection, they, like anyone, would have a hard time living with all of that personal rejection. The fact is, if prospective buyers don't buy from you, it's not a failure. The only failure that exists, if any, is if the seller fails to execute the needed actions required in a sale.

Blind attachment to the sales outcome is so pervasive that, many times, sales people will occupy themselves with mounds of menial tasks not associated with moving the Karmic sales needle. This busy work is often a Band-Aid used by them to internally help them justify why they are not selling. More often, the actions of the sales process would be much less work than it takes to create the illusion that they are not to blame.

We seek a place to hide, so we don't have to deal with the fears and hopes of what may or may not happen. It's a way for us to insulate ourselves and attempt to control our suffering. This shallow shelter is always temporary and will only lead to more suffering. Ultimately, we need to execute the needed actions and let go of the results from those actions.

The Bhagavad Gita says, "Those whose consciousness is unified abandon all attachment to the results of action and attain supreme peace. But those whose desires are fragmented, who are selfishly attached to the results of their work, are bound in everything they do." Our present actions, words, and thoughts are the only things that matter, so ask for the order.

CHAPTER 13
KARMIC NEGOTIATION
IN PRICING STRATEGY

The old axiom in the dominion of negotiation has long been, "If they bought your first offer, you should have asked for more money."

That principal is legitimate if "more money" equals a better opportunity for your prospective customer and a sage decision for their enterprise.

Another western philosophy regarding negotiation is "Neither party negotiating should feel good about the exchange once it's complete." This line of thinking presumes that both the seller and buyer were sitting across the bargaining table grinding and conceding point after point to get the best for themselves, leaving the other party without shelter in the face of winter.

The Venerable Geshe Kelsang Gyatso once said, "The solution to all the problems of daily life is to cherish others. All the happiness there is in the world arises from wishing others to be happy."

Walking into any negotiation with a prospective customer or client should be an opportunity to truly help them achieve what they are after. If a more daring investment in your product or service will indeed benefit all parties involved, begin your transaction with the largest product available to sell.

For example: Let's say you've reached the point of your sale when it's time for you to recommend a suite of products. Rather than offer a menu of items for the prospective buyer to pick and choose from, begin by offering all of your products and services.

The Rules of Karmic Negotiation do not start where a typical sales conversation begins. Most often, a typical sales dialogue includes a client-needs analysis that involves the seller asking how much the prospective buyer can afford. The seller then produces a menu of options for the customer. This is a flawed method on many levels.

First, we are turning over the leverage and reigns of the negotiation to one party, the buyer. Rather than offering what is right for them – regardless of price – and then waiting for a response, "yes" or "no," you are allowing them to make a choice based on price, not outcome. By letting the prospective client choose from a tiered menu according to component and price, or worse yet, packaging your product around what they can afford, you begin restricting opportunities for both parties.

So, how should we go about unveiling prices and items to a prospective buyer?

For this example, let's say we are a transactional, local, direct sales person. We'll use insurance as the product that we have to sell. Let's say we have four different packages:

*A platinum package that costs $1,500 per month and offers 10 different components of coverage.

*A gold package that costs $1,100 per month and offers seven different components of coverage.

*A silver package that costs $800 per month and offers four different components of coverage.

*A bronze package that costs $500 per month and offers two essential components of coverage.

Let's say you are talking to a couple who need insurance. They've indicated that they would best be served by a package that offers 10 components of coverage. You, as the seller, should then present, first and only, the platinum package.

Explain the coverage and components, provide the per-month price, ask them if they would like to buy it, and then stop talking. If they buy it, fill out the paperwork, take their payment, and thank them for the opportunity.

If they explain they can't afford the $1,500-per-month platinum package, do not ask, "How much can you afford?" Again, by turning the exchange into an endeavor of price, you confine the occasion for both the buyer and seller. Rather than asking what they can afford, move down to the next offering that closer reflects the expressed needs of the client. Explain, "I have another package, the gold package', that meets seven of the 10 coverage component requirements you requested, but it is more affordable than the platinum package. It's priced at $1,100 per month. Would you like to buy it?"

This Karmic shift of action has allowed us to be completely honest with the prospective clients about the fact that this package does not fulfill all of the required needs they've indicated, but it may be closer to what they can afford.

Let's say that the gold package is still too expensive for the prospective clients' budget.

The next appropriate step in Karmic Negotiation would be to present the silver package. Explain to them, "This silver package is much more modestly priced at $800 monthly; however, it fulfills only 4 of the 10 coverage components you indicated you desired. Would you like to buy it?"

Again, notice the full disclosure of the discrepancy about the client's needs and how it corresponds to a reduction of price. Also note that every time you unveil a new layer of this negotiation, a direct closing question is asked. Oftentimes, a seller will need to hear "no" five times before hearing "yes." Remember, there is nothing wrong with "no."

To conclude this illustration of Karmic Negotiation, let's say the prospective client says, "I still can't afford the silver package." Present the final package. Explain to them, "We do have a bronze package available that offers the two essential components of coverage. Clearly, this is a big disparity from the 10 coverage components you desired, but it is more economical. Would you like to buy it?"

If they prospective clients say "yes," you have earned a sale and offered a product that helped the clients come to an earnest and informed decision. If they say "no," at least you know you took as many actions as possible to manifest a sale. If they declined, then the reality was that they couldn't afford your product. Now you can focus your energy on helping someone else, and they can move on, as well.

Most often, if a client is interested, they will buy something you present before you get to the most modestly priced offering. If you were to simply produce a menu of tiered pricing and describe the differences, you lose the opportunity to ask for the order, which in and of it self will reduce the potency of your sales efforts. Furthermore, when it comes to menu pricing, most clients will always opt for the cheapest of the offerings. When it comes to insurance, advertising, and retirement funds, people are less concerned if they have the *right* product than they are more concerned with the fact that the have any product at all.

CHAPTER 14
THE PITCH – COMMISSION BREATH

There are many sage arguments about the presentation portion of selling, but I've found that not "selling" is the best possible way to pitch a product.

There's a phrase my longtime friend and mentor, Rob Skinner, says when he's coaching a burgeoning sales professional who really wants to make a sale. He calls the desperate act of over selling by newbies "commission breath."

Commission breath usually involves sales people who snuff out the fire of a sale because they broadcast the fact that they really need to make a sale. Common company with commission breath is a reiteration of the key points of offering, additional promises about the seller's commitment to the client, and a bumbled close.

Commission breath is the perfect term for this domain of desperation. The buyer can smell the anguish of the needy seller. Both usually want to flee, and as a rule, sellers with commission breath come up against clients who struggle to say "no" more often, because they are perceived as victims. As we discerned in early chapters, people want to help others in need. When prospective buyers tell commission-breathed sales people "I'll think about it," they think they're helping sellers foster hope, and they're hoping that the next people to come along will purchase something from those needy souls. Hope is nice, but it can't pay the light bill.

People also don't like to be "sold" anything. People like to trust others. Oftentimes, we as sales people feel we need to pick up the mantle of the carpet-bagging huckster, selling snake oil from town to town. I've never seen a snake oil salesman, but if I had to imagine one, his pitch would probably go something like this:

"Ladies and gentlemen step right up to buy this 'Des Moines - Snake Oil,' guaranteed to cure what ails you, including everything from shingles to yellow fever. Just one small capful of this miracle juice will make you run faster, dive deeper, and come up drier. It'll will improve your complexion and help with consumption. This is the phenomenal concoction that Chester A. Arthur took to cure his gout. Normally this sacred serum would cost $2,000 an ounce, but because of a mistake in ordering, we can sell it to you for just $19.99. If you buy it right now, I'll throw in an extra bottle!"

Now, lets compare that to a pitch I recently heard from an advertising sales person at a monthly magazine. Their names and locations have been changed to protect my car tires.

"Sir, thanks for taking the time to meet with us here at the Des Moines Chronicle. This ad schedule is sure to drive all sorts of new business through your doors. Our publication has a distribution of 115,000 people who read every inch of our magazine multiple times. As soon as they read your ad, they'll not only react, but they'll tell their friends. Our ads are also tax-deductible business investments, and there is nothing better for employee morale than to see your ad in the 'Des Moines Chronicle.' My customer, Al's Autos, routinely buys ads in our publication, and we're the reason he sells so many cars. Normally these beautiful full color advertisements cost $2,000, but because I'm in a rush to meet my goal, my boss has authorized me to sell this to you for just $400. If you tell me 'yes' right now, I'll throw in free design!"

Confucius once said, "The superior man understands what is right; the inferior man understands what will sell." I suggest you simply sell the right stuff.

The pitch from the snake oil salesman and the magazine rep are eerily similar to each other, yes? I actually transcribed the ad rep's pitch, verbatim.

If you're a businessperson who deals with ad reps, you've probably heard a pitch that was very similar to the one from the magazine rep at some point. It feels sleazy, because it is.

I've found that sales people who migrate toward this desperate huckster approach are afflicted with the same symptoms.

1. They lack confidence in themselves.
2. They lack belief in the effectiveness of the product they're selling.
3. They generally sell small sized packages for low dollar amounts.
4. They live a miserable life drowning in perturbation of what they do at work.

Why do sales people who oversell the pitch have these symptoms? Let's go point by point.

Lack of confidence in one's self is nothing more than a manifestation of fear. Lack of confidence in ourselves is caused by our fear of being intrusive, a fear of seeming to be manipulative, or the fear of not producing a sale. The strange thing is, those fears only make sales people with that lack of confidence embrace a mousey intrusive nature and a manipulative style of selling, and usually, they don't bring about sales because of commission breath.

Lack of belief in the product is always connected to offering smaller sized packages for low dollar amounts. Essentially, because sellers don't fully believe in the product they are selling, they become more comfortable selling smaller packages, because, if the product isn't all that the seller said it would be, at least the buyer won't be out too much money.

If sales people know their products or services have a lower level of quality than they claim, then they are lying. If people buy those lies, then the sellers are stealing.

If a seller who doesn't believe the product they are representing works, they will sell smaller packages more often. A subconscious justification takes place in which the doubting seller decides to burden more people with smaller amounts stolen. This way (in the eyes of the uncertain seller) no one or two buyers have the burden of paying a lot of money, and the sales person isn't committing grand larceny. Again, this is generally an underlying notion that sales people probably wouldn't even recognize. They would never say, "This is why I only peddle small packages." Obviously, if sales people are committing acts of petty larceny and they know it, it's a challenge to show up day after day to do a job they feel is dishonest.

If you have read this passage and found that you fit the description of this kind of sales person, then it's time to do two things. First, educate yourself as much as you can about the product or service you're selling. Second, if it doesn't live up to what you claim or are asked to claim, ask yourself if you can continue being dishonest with yourself and with others.

So, we've dissected how and why many pitches go pear

shaped. Let's examine how to get our pitches right. Depending on what it is you're selling, most products and offers can be concisely illustrated in less than two minutes time. Identify all of the core benefits and how they reflect any of the concerns or needs your clients indicated in prior conversations. State your well-rehearsed bullet points clearly and with confidence, and then ask your closing question. Don't over do it.

Remember, no one likes to be "sold," so don't sell; rather, present. Follow these tips.

- Make good eye contact with everyone in the room.
- Dress for success. If you were a rancher, you wouldn't hire a farmhand who wore a flip-flops. Look as professional as you plan to act.
- Show up on time. No excuses for being late. Also, don't turn up early; people hate that.
- Keep your promise on the amount of time requested for your presentation. Busy people budget their time; don't go long, because you are costing them time and money, which is a possible indication of what you may do with their business.
- Make your presentation documents as professional-looking as possible. This is one of the points you can prepare for. Remember, preparation plus opportunity equals luck.

CHAPTER 15
THE BRUCE LEE CLOSE

Martial artist and author Bruce Lee once said, "I fear not the man who has practiced 10,000 kicks once, but I fear the man who has practiced one kick 10,000 times."

In the course of coaching thousands of sales people of all makes and models, I have been confounded again and again to learn that, most often, they do not rely on standard, well-rehearsed verbiage when asking for the order.

On occasions when I've probed sellers for their justifications, most say they don't have a standardized close because of something similar to the following logic: "Every customer is different, and I like to keep my reaction to them different."

In the earlier chapter "Asking for the Order," we discussed the failure of many sales people when it comes to actually asking people if they would like to buy. Preparing a rehearsed closing question allows a muscle memory-like function to take place in your sale.

To learn more about Bruce Lee's muscle memory philosophy about "practicing one kick 10,000 times," I sought out practitioners of the martial arts style called Jeet Kune Do.

Jeet Kune Do is a practical mode of self defense developed by Lee. At first, this discipline was met with great skepticism from the masters of other disciplines and protocols with lineage that dated back thousands of years. Jeet Kune Do barked directly in the face of the principles of most of the major martial arts regimes.

The Jeet Kune Do teacher who instructed me said that unlike other martial arts that remain rigidly focused on rank, standards and belts, the brainchild of Bruce Lee concentrates on executing the right actions in situations that people would most often *react* to emotionally. Rather than making it's students reach a bar under the scrutiny of others, like in other heritage martial arts, Jeet Kune Do's aim is for each individual practitioner to remain lucid in the face of turmoil and to be able to summon the proper reaction for each occasion.

Though at first traditional martial arts masters discounted Lee and this alien discipline, Jeet Koon Do went on to be one of the core curriculums for many branches of the U.S. Special Forces. It's also practiced and utilized by many law enforcement agencies across America.

In the series of training sessions I attended, I learned a technique called "brush-grab-punch." This technique involved me, the defender, countering a punch from an attacker by brushing the attacker's punching hand away with my lead hand, grabbing the attacker's brushed hand with my opposite hand, and then pulling them close to me while I clenched my lead hand (the one that I had brushed with) and delivered one of Bruce Lee's famous one-inch punches somewhere on the body or face of the attacker.

At first, the technique was taught to me very slowly. Though I felt I could go faster, the instructor deliberately made me take my time, repeating the drill over and over again. We drilled the brush-grab-punch technique for over an hour on one hand, gradually getting faster until the three maneuvers were one, and I could focus on power and speed. Then, we repeated the process with the other hand for the next hour. I was physically exhausted, but I owned that technique. I was no longer thinking about what to do and when I needed to do it. In fact, I wasn't thinking at all. I was simply allowing muscle memory to do its thing.

This ability to summon the proper response in the face of turmoil is exactly what sculpting and drilling the perfect closing question allows a seller to do in the face of turmoil.

Turmoil? Yes, if you remember from previous chapters we talked about a subtle remnant of the "fight-or-flight" response that is evoked in any sales negotiation. Even when someone wants to buy something from you, that bargaining communication activates a prewired fear of conflict.

Whether we like to admit it or not, the feelings of fear, anxiety, and trepidation flood our minds. This, in turn, fills our bloodstream with adrenaline when it comes time to ask for the order. This reaction happens to all kinds of sellers, from rookies to well-weathered vets.

In Chapter 7, "Hard to Say No," we talked about the fear buyers face when it comes to rejecting sellers. When you compound the fear experienced by buyers with the fear experienced by sellers, it's a wonder any commerce happens at all! Buddha said this about fear: "The whole secret of existence is to have no fear. Never fear what will become of you; depend on no one. Only the moment when you reject all help are you freed."

The day will come in your sales career when you will have that enlightened notion that Buddha professed over 2,500 years ago, and fear will not be an issue. But until then, take a cue from Bruce Lee, and summon an emotion-free response to a situation and brush-grab-punch, meaning develop and drill your own closing question.

Every closing question should be brief, and it should cut

right to the bone of the matter. Most importantly, it should be a question; not a statement.

In many business-to-business sales people whom I've coached, I've seen many realize success with the simple closing question, "Will you trust me with your business for the next year?" Or with, "If you'll just authorize this, I'll get going on what I do best." Either way, make it your own, and like Bruce Lee, drill-drill-drill.

Many times, prospective buyers will say "yes" to a closing question, but not endorse whatever agreement you have at the time you're offering the closing question. This usually occurs when their courage fails them at a time when they should say "no," or when they are too sheepish to object to certain points of your presentation. Addressing those objections also requires disciplined practice.

CHAPTER 16
ADDRESSING OBJECTIONS

If you have you ever seen a presidential debate, then you'll be familiar with this scene: two grown men standing at neighboring podiums trying to trump each other with 10-second sound bites, an over abundance of swagger and a lot of spin. Never in the history of United States presidential debates has one of the candidates listened thoughtfully to an opponent's stance on an issue and said, "Wow, I was all wrong about that issue – I've changed my mind!" Many sellers get caught up in having a debate with prospective clients. In sales, nobody wins a debate. Oftentimes, we are concerned with overcoming objections when we should be addressing concerns and solving problems with the buyer

If we can understand precisely what is keeping prospective buyers from doing business with us, we can more effectively *make action happen faster*. All of the possible objections that would restrict sales are only variations of the four primary objections:

1. The prospective buyer has more questions.

2. The prospective buyer wants to haggle.

3. The prospective buyer wants a shorter length of term in the agreement.

4. The prospective buyer needs assurance that you, or your product, will do all you claim.

First, to the questions. Most often, clients who have questions don't articulate these questions well. If there are questions remaining, it means you, as the seller, didn't do a good enough job in pitching the product.

For this example, let's say your closing question is, "That's my offer. Now will you trust me with your business for the next year?" For argument's sake, let's say your client's response is, "I don't know." What they are saying without saying is one of two things:

1. "I lack the precise tools to properly communicate my questions."

2. "I don't have the courage to tell you no."

No matter which of those two statements is what they really mean to say, your response should be the same.

1. Restate their objection.

2. Empathize with the objection.

3. Probe deeper to isolate the true objection.

For example, when the prospective buyer replies to, "Will you trust me with your business for the next year?" by saying, "I don't know," respond first by restating their response: "I understand that you don't have an answer right now." Second, empathize with them: "There is a lot to consider." Third, probe deeper and isolate their true objection: "So I can most effectively help you, what are you unsure about – is it the term or the price?" This will, without question, lead you to a position where you can respond to the individual concerns one at a time. If your product will ultimately pay for itself, include that in the rebuttal to "price." If the term is the objection and your product is priced at that rate because of the length of commitment, articulate that. No matter what the chief objection is, you must help them become clearer than, "I don't know."

If the prospective buyer wants to haggle on price, they are saying one of two things.

1. I can't afford it.

2. I don't believe in the value you are claiming.

For example, if you strike the closing question, "Will you trust me with your business for the next year?" and they reply with, "I like the components, but I just don't like the price." Follow the same steps as before. First, restate their objection: "So if I understand you correctly, it's the right product, but the price is your chief concern?" Second, empathize with them: "In this economy, every penny counts." Third, probe deeper and isolate the true concern: "So I'm crystal clear, do you like the product and simply cannot afford it, or can you afford my product and do not feel it's worthy of the price I'm asking?"

Here's what to do if the answer is, "I can't afford it:" Unless yours is a product that allows clients to generate more money, consider collecting a "no" and moving on. Again, our job as sales people is not to get people to do things they don't want to or shouldn't do – our job is to *make action happen faster*. In some cases, "no" is an appropriate answer.

Here's what to do if the answer is, "I don't think your product is worthy of the price:" Restate the core benefits of the product and restate the close and confidently ask for the order again.

Most objections are really about the prospective buyer needing reassurance that something will work, so confidently and professionally speak to the benefits and again ask for the money. Remember, how they respond is out of our control; the only thing we can control is if we ask and how we ask.

"The World Best Negotiator," Herb Cohen, is best known for ironing out terms for everything from hostile corporate takeovers to hostage crisis situations. Cohen has a phrase he first told me in 2006: "Care, but not that much." Essentially, Cohen's philosophy suggests that we offer our product and let go of the result. I think this is the perfect approach when handling objections. Remember "no" is always better than "maybe".

CHAPTER 17
WORKRATE - EXCUSES

In the Chatham Islands of the South Pacific exist a people called the Moriori. Anthropologists estimate that these pacifist fishermen first arrived with their evolving traditions at least 600 years ago.

Until recently, this coastal culture relied heavily on the daily catch from the sea to feed their families and contribute to their villages. Each Moriari patriarch would take small boats called Tainui from the coast of the Chatham Islands to nearby reefs loaded with vast varieties of fish. At the end of every day, they'd return to their families with their catch – that night's dinner and breakfast and lunch for the next day.

Like any sales endeavor, there was no guarantee of success for these fishermen. They faced the dynamics of the tide, unpredictable spawning patterns, weather, and a whole host of factors out of their control that cause sporadic slumps and streaks in their ongoing fishing excursions.

For example, let's say a fictional Moriori fisherman hit a slump where he didn't manage to collect enough fish for his large extended family of 15. This family relied on the fruits of this fisherman's labor, and for two weeks, the fisherman and his family had gone with less and less food because of the slump.

The fisherman was growing concerned about the shortfall. Anxiety and doubt plagued him and his efforts to collect fish. The angst caused the Moriori fisherman to second-guess himself and make poor decisions about what to fish for, where to fish, and when to fish. He became desperate and uneasy. No matter what the fisherman did, he failed to catch enough fish. Despite the fact that others around him caught what they needed, he failed day after day.

At some point in the continuing toil, the fisherman made a trip to his village shaman. Rather than blessing the fisherman's nets or fishing grounds, or praying for a turn in weather, the fictive shaman guided the fisherman on an introspective journey into what was going wrong.

Obviously there were enough fish in the sea, so fruitless excuses pointed outward would not help fill the man's boat or the bellies of his family.

The answer to collecting more fish is spending more time fishing instead of placing blame, or reacting to scarcity by trying new and desperate tactics. The fisherman needs to simply spend more time on the water.

On average the fictional fisherman spent eight hours a day angling. If he simply invested one more hour in the morning, and one more hour at the end of the day striving to catch fish, his odds increase by 25 percent. At this point, a 10 hour work day that resulted in 25 percent more fish would be a welcome exchange compared to the 8 hour days filled with disappointment, anxiety, fear, and the sorrow felt by walking into his home without enough for everyone at the end of the day.

It's not as simple as working two more hours a day in the face of a slump, though. "Fish more" would be an obvious solution that would have certainly occurred to the weary fisherman long before the trip to the shaman. So why didn't he just bookend each day's work with one more hour?

Something was hindering the drive of the fisherman. That something is not found on the water or with his failing hooks. His internal motivation wasn't enough to compel him to increase his work rate. This is why the shaman initiated the meditative contemplation exercise. The shaman and the fisherman grasp that if they can find clarity, rid and the fisherman of anxiety, fear, and doubt, then they can likely take a step toward the renewal of the fisherman's passion for fishing and providing.

Slumps in sales will inevitably occur. When they do, we as sales people – like the fisherman – often begin to make desperate decisions and react to perceived failures with fear. This fear is one of the principal forces limiting our drive and desire to try harder.

In sales, there are countless variables that change the dynamics of our success. When faced with declining sales, our natural instinct is to attempt to control these variables. Striving to control anything only leads to disappointment and suffering.

Coexisting with the suffering caused by vain attempts to control the ungovernable is the realm of excuses. Some sellers who fail to sell habitually point to the economy, the weather, seasonal events, and failings of the product.

Rather than making frenzied attempts to call on new clientele in foreign markets with all new closing questions and differing products, or by plying the world with excuses, simply increase your work rate. Like the fictional Moriori Fisherman, this has probably already occurred to you.

So what is then that is limiting you from increasing your sales attempts by 25 percent simply by working an extra hour on either side of your eight-hour day? Most sales slumps would succumb to a simple 25 percent increase in productivity. But it's more than just "working harder."

What is at the core of our desire not to get an early start and end the day a bit later?

For all of us, every slump is different. The answers to bleak motivation *reside inside*. By meditating with a specific focus on renewing your motivation and detaching from perceived failure, you'll find freedom from fear. The simple desire to renew your excitement for work is a first step toward actually finding pleasure in your work. At first, focus on single steps, not mile-long sprints, in this renewal. Confucius once said, "It does not matter how slowly you go so long as you do not stop."

If we can find an opportunity in the obstacle of a slump, then we have released the power the slump holds over us.

CHAPTER 18
EVOKE EMOTION

Buddha once said, "Thousands of candles can be lit by a single candle."

I'm certain Buddha wasn't thinking about fueling commerce via advertising, email marketing or social media, but that incisive phrase about inspiring others through actions and words dovetails perfectly with the ability to duplicate a sale process with an emotion-evoking communication.

It's been said that success in sales is the ability to duplicate a sales process. Whether we're talking about re-using a sales method that succeeded on subsequent sales calls; or hiring other sellers, training them to take a sales process to a multitude of direct sales prospects; or advertising our goods or services to the masses, it's all about the duplication of a sales process. By doing that, we are inspiring others with our actions or words.

Those words must be economical, sensible and, most importantly, evoke emotions.

Most entrepreneurs and sales people will have to manage an advertising campaign in one form or another. Many people misunderstand the goal and purpose of an ad campaign. This is why many have a critical outlook on advertising, because there are boundless ways to get it wrong. Today there are so many ways to effectively communicate with prospective customers, from terrestrial methods, such as TV, radio, print and outdoor, to new, more intuitive advertising methods, such as email marketing, social media, and digital geo-targeting apps, the latter of which can track your location from a store and intuitively tailor an advertisement to your past purchases and personal demographics. No matter what means you use, all advertisements are designed to do the exact thing. It's the same thing all sales are meant to do, and that is to *make action happen faster*.

In its simplest sense, all advertising is a referral from one being to another that something, and somewhere is safe. As human beings, we require this referral because we are inherently wired to be weary of the unknown. That same weariness has kept us alive generation after generation.

Let's go back in time to the hills of Southern France. Assume for a moment there exists a family of cave men, women, and children in search of shelter from a volatile, Ice Age, winter day. It's snowing and raining heavily, and the wind is blowing sideways. This family must soon find protection from the storm. Suddenly, they come across a cavern. It's big, deep and dark. Do they go in? Chances are, no they won't go in, because lurking at the back of that cavern could be a giant bear, or another Ice Age mega-predator, ready to eat them.

Chances are, that family will keep searching for shelter that is clearly safer. But then, just before the family moves on, a second family emerges from the big, deep, dark cave and they say, "Hey, come on in! There are no bears in here. We've got a bunch of berries, and this new thing we've found? We call it 'fire,' you're gonna love it!" Suddenly, the invisible barrier keeping the first cave family out has been eliminated. That referral from one being to another has prompted action.

Every business has an invisible barrier that exists at the threshold of their door. Use your own experience. Is there a place, a restaurant perhaps, you've driven by day after day, year after year. For whatever reason, you've never gone in. People are actually more apt to go back to a restaurant in which they've had a bad dining experience instead of going to a new restaurant they haven't experienced. Emotion-evoking advertisements are an effective way to break down those invisible barriers.

There is a famous quote by the founder of Revlon Cosmetics, Charles Revson, that goes, "In the factory, we make cosmetics; in the drugstore, we sell hope." Revson understood that when it came to communicating to prospective buyers, he could list all of the pedestrian details about his company's cosmetics, or he could solve his prospective customer's problems with his products. He could make every woman who bought his product more beautiful, so that is what he sold. What would you buy? A bunch of chemicals mashed together in a bottle that you're supposed to put on your face, or the hope of looking more beautiful?

So often, businesses mistakenly make themselves or their products the subjects of their advertisements. The people who are subjected to our advertisements do not care about us. They care about solutions to their problems. If you can solve their problems, then your ad will be more effective.

I wish I could have a one-on-one consultation with every insurance salesman who puts his headshot on a billboard. I'm sure you've seen these billboards. They usually are positioned on a busy roadside and feature a forgettable picture of a guy's head and torso wearing a tie. This picture is usually next to his ordinary name and a phone number printed in type that's too small, as if people driving 65 mph in bumper-to-bumper traffic would really be looking for a pen and paper to write down the number.

Or how about the local car dealer ads on TV?

They usually feature the owner of the dealership in a poorly fitting suit making awkward hand gestures that don't correspond to the verbiage. Usually, these guys say "folks," "low financing," and "come on down." Do you really think people are sitting at home saying to themselves, "Well, I'm convinced – there has never been a better time to buy from that dealer. I mean did you see his hand gestures!"

The reason these sales people mistakenly make their ads about them and not about the solutions their customers require is they're led down this path by poorly trained ad reps. Ad reps have long asked their clients to "voice their own ads," in part because they know their client's friends will likely say, "I heard you on the radio!" And though they are getting feedback, the bulk of the audience has tuned that advertisement out, because it evokes no emotion and solves none of the client's problems. This is a severe waste of money and time; it pointlessly strokes egos and does little to make action happen faster.

When it comes to the content of your advertisement, the riskiest thing you can do is to blend in with the other ads. You must be different.

But how do you find to the right message for you?

CHAPTER 19
IT'S ALL ABOUT THEM

When attempting to develop the proper message for your business, follow these four steps.

1. Identify your unique selling proposition.

2. Identify the emotion that compels your customers to do business with you.

3. Build a slogan based around that unique selling proposition and emotion.

4. Build a campaign around that slogan.

When working to determine your unique selling proposition, list all of the benefits from every product or service you offer. Then pragmatically rank those until you've identified why the bulk of your customers come to you first and keep coming back. If you have a restaurant, perhaps you offer a steak that people have been known to drive 100 miles for. If you have a pet shop, perhaps it's you're expansive inventory. If you have a computer repair shop, it could be that it's the only shop in your neighborhood that will work on Macs. What is the one key reason why your customers choose to do business with you over your competition?

After you've identified your unique selling proposition, find the emotion that compels your customers to come through the door. If you operate a bar, it could be "fun." If you own a strip bar, it might be "lust." If you have a café and have identified your pies as your unique selling proposition, "hunger" would be the appropriate emotion. Not every emotion has to be connected to your industry.

What do the humorous Caveman campaigns from Geico have to do with insurance? Nothing, but Geico (The Martin Agency) effectively used humor to successfully differentiate themselves from a crowded field of insurance companies that were already using the emotion of "security" in a their ads, for example, "You're in good hands with Allstate."

Slogans are essential to building a strong campaign. They help your prospective customers recognize you in a competitive field. They communicate why people need your products or services, and they aid in recall.

The best slogans are no longer than two to four words in length, they can contain your core product or service offerings in the slogan, and they reflect the attitude of your business, for example, Nike's (Weiden + Kennedy) "Just do it" suggests action needs to happen – stop procrastinating and get it done – all while suggesting a swagger and strut from this brand. These three simple words, "Just do it," communicate all of those things and more, and Nike has ridden on the back of that simple message since 1988.

Again, it is critical that the slogans we develop from the unique selling proposition and the emotion that compels customers to come through the door be about out customers, not us or our businesses.

In 2007, Walmart made a great leap forward with their brand. For 19 years of their company's history, their slogan was "Always low prices, always." This slogan was clearly about Walmart, not Walmart's customers. And it was dead wrong. Walmart faced a barrage of public criticisms, such as, "Walmart turns small towns into ghost towns," "low prices, means cheap," "They're not taking care of their employees," or "Most of their products are made in China." The astounding thing was Walmart paid someone to paint the company with the wrong positioning statement, which perpetuated the perception problems.

Walmart certainly needed a facelift.

Walmart tapped Global Insight, which in turn contracted, The Martin Agency (the ad ninjas who conceived the brilliant Geico campaigns) to help come up with a new slogan to help revive consumer confidence in the world's largest retailer. Their efforts produced "Save Money. Live Better." An eloquent, four-word statement that communicated the benefits to the customer and ceased the incessant dialogue about Walmart. In one swift move, Walmart went from "cheap" to helping their customers "save money," and, with the money they save and the products they found at Walmart, "live better."

If Walmart, Global Insight, and The Martin Agency were to have followed the rules of developing a slogan, they would have identified Walmart's unique selling proposition, which is "affordability." You certainly can find better products at other retailers, but it is very hard to compete with Walmart on price.

Walmart then took their identified unique selling proposition of "affordability" and found an emotion with which their consumers would identify. Obviously, if people can be frugal in the face of a recession or down economy, they can stretch their limited resources. They can sustain abundance for themselves and their family. This affirmative notion has served Walmart well.

Another key mistake businesses make when it comes to crafting a slogan is highlighting their own perceived strengths versus their competition. In most advertising, it's best not to acknowledge your competition at all, let alone their shortcomings; rather focus on how we can help our prospective customers by solving their problems.

The Dalai Lama once said, "We are all the same human being with the same potential to be a good human being or a bad human being. The important thing is to realize the positive side and try to increase that; realize the negative side and try to reduce. That's the way."

This philosophy heralded by the Dalai Lama was proven right in the 2008 United States presidential election. Take a look at the campaign branding.

The 2008 McCain-Palin campaign slogans turned out to be an amalgam of various sound bites and talking points. McCain and Palin positioned themselves as "mavericks," taking a ride on "The Straight Talk Express." Their official campaign slogans were "Reform, prosperity and peace" and "Country first." It was hard for Americans to pin down precisely what the McCain/Palin ticket intended in their choppy, disorganized array of taglines. Also, all of those campaign position statements fragmented the focus of the McCain constituents and acknowledged his opponents and predecessors (even though that acknowledgement was negative.)

Look at the term "mavericks," for instance, which insinuates that while *everyone else* running for president will fall in line with the party's agenda, McCain and Palin will do their own thing.

The problem is, this angle highlights *everyone else* running, not the needs of the American people. Same goes for "The Straight Talk Express." This insinuates that while *everyone else* will bamboozle you with jargon and statistics, McCain and Palin will render it down in plain English. Finally,

"Reform, prosperity and peace." Having watched non-stop political coverage of the presidential race in 2007-2008 I was surprised to learn that was one of their slogans. Frankly, I feel it was veiled behind all of the others. To me, the "prosperity and peace" part of the slogan speaks to the needs of the voting Americans, but "Reform" puts emphasis and power on the existing governing forces, or *everyone else* who has been running the country.

Meanwhile, in the Obama-Biden camp, they featured two of their most prominent, sweet-and-simple slogans. Both were affirmations that spoke to the needs of Americans. "Hope" and "Yes, we can."

"Hope" was self-explanatory after the American recession that economists said started somewhere between 2006 to 2007. Also, many Americans hoped for peace in the face of two trying and costly foreign wars initiated during the previous administration. None of the power of that slogan was devoted to the energy of blaming George W. Bush; instead, it was devoted to optimism for the future. In the core Obama-Biden slogan "Yes, we can," "Yes" is an affirmation, "we," is inclusive of all, and "can" is a statement of capability.

The 2012 presidential campaign saw the Obama-Biden ticket succeed again with an even shorter affirmation about the American people's needs – the slogan "Forward." Some of the best advertising is devoted to reinforcing positive decisions made by your existing customers. It's always easier to get someone to come back to your business than it is to persuade a new customer to try your business. Preach to the choir about what the choir needs.

To some, slogans seem like a nice summary sentiment, but it's more than that. Those words hold power, the power to affect action and lead to change.

A routine mistake made by many advertisers after building the perfect slogan is to build a campaign that does not reflect the slogan. Many times, in working with hometown merchants, I'll find advertisements that feature layers of prices, items, and arguments about how great their sales staff is or the fact that they are "locally owned and operated." A good songwriter builds the hook of the song and then builds the rest of the song around that hook. The same approach should be taken when assembling your campaign.

The campaign or advertisement should rigidly be informed by the slogan you've developed. This is why it's so important to identify your unique selling proposition, find the perfect emotion to evoke, and develop a flawless slogan for your brand.

CHAPTER 20
MANTRA ADVERTISING

In my time of guiding over 1,600 advertising campaigns, I've learned a simple but powerful truth: "Repetition builds recall, and recall drives decisions." How repetition is achieved is a matter that confounds many business people and sales people alike.

Indian Yogi and Spiritual Guru Paramahansa Yogananda once said, "It is better to say just one phrase repeating it vigorously from low to high or high to whisper and lastly from a whisper to mental affirmations until one feels what he is saying, i.e., repeating a phrase with varying depth of soul-feeling until one realizes the meaning of his utterance in every fiber of his being."

Yogananda was certainly talking about the benefits of repeating an affirmative mantra, not advertisements, right? Hold on! Let's define "mantra":

mantra |'mantrə, 'män-| (noun), A statement uttered repetitiously to aid in concentration and considered capable of creating transformation.

Good advertisements are nothing more than statements uttered repetitiously with the aim to inform a prospective customer base and influence action.

When Yogananda says repeating a phrase vigorously helps one realize the meaning, he's applying the advertising principal that repetition reinforces. As youngsters, we learn the alphabet, because someone was kind enough to repeat the letters to us over and over again. Adults were even thoughtful enough to include a little musical branding to help insure our recall. If our guardians were to recite to us the profound gift of the alphabet only once, it truly wouldn't be a gift. It would be a waste of both the parents' time and the children's time.

Many advertisers attempt to influence sales with a message that is compelling, different, and that evokes the right emotion that identifies with their customers' needs, but too often, there is simply not enough repetition behind it.

To get at the core of effective advertising placement, we need to discern the two types of advertising. Now, there is an array of forms of advertising. There's email, TV, radio social media, outdoor signage, direct mail, directory listings, etc. But I'm talking about the two ways to implement advertising across all spectrums:

1. Promotional spike advertising

2. Recall awareness advertising.

Promotional spike is not for every business. It is for businesses that employ special events, sales, and short-term offers. Most often, these categories include restaurants, retailers, car dealerships, grocery stores, or any business that offers a finite price for a limited amount of time. A few examples of promotional spike advertisements would be the "Cash for Clunkers" campaign. From July 24, 2009, until Aug. 24 2009, American vehicle owners could participate in the Car Allowance Rebate System, which allowed them to receive $3,500 to $4,500 on their trades, provided they met basic criteria, and the money could be put toward newer, more fuel-efficient vehicles. The rules were simple: Act within this window of time, and you'll be able to enjoy the benefit of a better deal on your trade.

Another example would be the McDonald's Monopoly

campaign. For a limited time, once a year, McDonald's rolls out an incentive that leads to many prizes for their customers. McDonald's uses promotional spike advertisements often, but only when they have a strong level of recall awareness advertising in place. You'll only ever see a "McRib is back" campaign, or "The shamrock shake returns" commercial alongside other recall-based ads from McDonald's that repetitiously keep that brand and the slogan "I'm lovin' it" in the front of our minds.

Having a base level of recall is essential before attempting to engage in promotional spike advertising. Why? Because promotional spike advertising by itself often lacks the longevity, continuity, or repetition to effectively drive recall and in turn drive decisions.

A great example of how promotional spike advertising fails without a strong base of recall occurred during the 2006 Super Bowl. That year, the Seattle Seahawks lost to the Pittsburgh Steelers on ABC in front of an estimated television audience of 90.6 million viewers, or just over 30 percent of the United States population at the time. The Super Bowl is the one time of the year when people don't flip past the commercials or zone out. The viewers are actively vested in the ads. It's the one time a year when advertisers can shine! That's why Magnolia Pictures bought a 30 second ad for an estimated $2.6 million for their major motion picture "The Worlds Fastest Indian," starring Anthony Hopkins as a motorcycle builder that beats the land speed record. It's a pretty good flick. The problem is I'm one of the few who watched it, and I didn't get around to it until 2010. This box office disaster only managed to gross a paltry $5.13 Million at box office. The cost to make the film plus the cost of the ineffective advertisement resulted in a horrible loss for the studio. If we're really generous and say that half of those ticket sales came from that Super Bowl ad, this means that ad managed to influence less than .3 percent of the millions of people who were exposed to the $2.6 million ad.

Magnolia Films was banking on a bigger fraction of the 90.6 million viewers to react to the message. But they didn't.

Why?

Because this commercial lacked the type of repetition required to drive recall and in turn drive decisions. It aired one time. I call this the "Super Bowl Mistake." In fact, the Super Bowl ad schedule is a revolving grave yard of failed brands that thought they could drive decisions without a an established base of recall or required repetition, brands like Computers.com, PS Cleaner, and many others that obviously weren't familiar with Yogananda's advice about "repeating a phrase until one realizes the meaning of his utterance in every fiber of his being."

There are many successful brands that command the formidable Super Bowl audience, brands such as Budweiser and Bridgestone Tires, but these brands all have a strong level of recall awareness in place with the core NFL football audience before they engage in promotional spike advertising. Follow their lead with your business. Avoid buying the limited-time offer ad schedule, the "game of the week," or the 90-day ad package that ad reps often schlep.

Let's take a look at another form of competition. The re-election rate for incumbent U.S. congressional office holders over the past 10 years ranges between 83 and 96 percent. Why is this? Surely with all of the corrupt and bad politicians out there, there must be more than 4 to 17 percent of the challengers who could do a better job! The fact is, many of the challengers who run against incumbent office holders are probably better suited to hold office. But, because of the dynamics of recall, we never vote for them. There may be a bear lurking at the back of that cave. Think about it: The present office holder has years to shake everyone's hand, kiss every baby, sign scores of bills, and put their names on hundreds of press releases. These incumbents are building a strong level of recall awareness before they attempt to engage in promotional spike advertising during the primary or general elections. Essentially, the challengers, unless they have a modicum of established name recognition, are left to make the "Super Bowl Mistake."

How then, should we engage in recall advertising? First, I recommend you do research on your market and the advertising mediums available to you. Find the medium that commands the largest segment of your target and prospective customer base.

Check references of existing advertisers – listen, view, or read to find out who they are. See what they have to say about the local medium they're using; don't just make a decision by what the ad rep says. Also, check your ad rep's credentials. If they're worth their salt, they will be a strong ally for your business for a long time.

Next, avoid the "spray and pray" approach. Many small business owners make the large mistake of buying several small campaigns on varying media and, in essence, fail to drive enough recognition on any one medium.

It's much better to communicate a single message 500 times to 500 people than it is to communicate a single message five times to 50,000 people. The five-times-to-50,000-people scenario is essentially a smaller version of the "Super Bowl Mistake." Rather, take a laser-focused approach and communicate with the segment of your prospective consumer base that you can afford to speak with repetitiously. If you do not have a budget to talk to 80 percent of the segment of your market, scale down your budget and speak to 60 percent, 40 percent, 20 percent or 5 percent.

Whatever you do, do not cease the dialogue, even with that 5 percent. Sustain that communication with that segment of your existing and prospective customer base for the duration of time you're in business. When that conversation with that 5 percent has garnered a "return on investment," that is when you take a step forward (if you're ready) and talk to a larger percentage of your market, and that is how some of America's best businesses managed to grow in the face of the worst economic downturn since the Great Depression: one foot in front of the other.

CHAPTER 21
THE LEAK AND IMPERMANENCE

So, after you've found the right emotion-evoking message and you've found the right medium, when can you take a break? Japanese Zen Buddhist Teacher Dogen Zenji said this about impermanence: "Your body is like a dew drop on the morning grass, your life is as brief as a flash of lightning. Momentary and vain, it is lost in a moment." Awareness about your products from a base of prospective customers is also fleeting.

Sustaining a level of achieved customer awareness is as important as sustaining the flow of electricity to your shop. In advertising, there is a powerful dynamic always at work that requires you to consistently replenish customer awareness. This dynamic is called "the leak." The leak can be assessed with a deluge of equations that take into account your market size, demographics, and more, but essentially, it can be filtered down to bullet points.

The leak, in its simplest form, represents a loss in customer awareness, and it's caused by three factors:

1. People naturally forget.

2. Migration to and from your market.

3. Competitors gaining mind share.

People forgetting is obvious. Without repeatedly singing the alphabet to children, they will fail to remember the ABCs.

Depending on your city, your market's turnover could be as little as 10 percent of the population – that includes people moving in, moving away, dying, or coming of age to use your products or services. In some severe cases, such as college towns or cities with military bases, turnover could be as high as 30 percent. This would mean 30 percent of the people whom you have educated about your product or service are leaving your market, never to use your business again. And 30 percent of the incoming crowd has absolutely no knowledge of you or your business. Even if yours is a heritage business that has been in town for 100 years, perceptually, you're on the same footing as a new business just starting out in your community.

Beating the competition means gaining mind share and, in turn, market share. The Government Employees Insurance Company was founded in 1936 in Fort Worth, Texas, with a mission to provide auto insurance directly to federal government employees and their families. For most of the company's modest existence, it was not a major player in the world of insurance companies in America, until that is, they leveraged the "Geico Gecko" campaign in 1999. From that time to now, Geico has managed to take mind share and market share away from well established brands, like Allstate, State Farm, and Farmers, that failed to keep pace with Geico's aggressive bids for business. By 2007, Geico insured more than 13 Million cars, and it continues to consistently rank among the top five car insurance companies in America. Geico did a better job sustaining and replenishing customer awareness than its competitors., and so the company attracted the customers other insurance companies lost through natural turnover rates – Geico took advantage of the leak.

CHAPTER 22
FREQUENCY, NOT FREQUENTLY

When I was a teenager, I took a job as a disc jockey at a low-watt, AM radio station on the outskirts of a rural, prairie town. In addition to hourly log readings from a gigantic radiating transmitter (which is surely why I'm a bit bent today), one of my duties included recording "Paul Harvey's News and Comment" on a single-track cart. The feed was sent down after a couple of cue tones from the ABC satellite. Every day, I would record and then play back the show. I would also repeat this process for the "Paul Harvey's The Rest of the Story." Each day was the same; I'd wait for the cues, record the two programs, and then monitor them as they played back on the air.

Within one year's time, I listened to Paul Harvey a minimum of 1,000 times. Even though we had a very small audience, its members were extremely loyal and passionately vocal on the rare occasion when I'd miss the tones and cut off part of the show. I learned quickly that there was a very devout audience of Paul Harvey zealots who made a daily appointment to tune into this product.

In the monotony of being subjected to America's most beloved radio personality, I noticed that Paul Harvey had the same consistent advertiser day after day, show after show – Citracal.

If you're not acquainted with Citracal, it is a bone density supplement that offers, according to its advertisements, "unsurpassed absorption of calcium citrate and Vitamin D-3." This meant nothing to me; obviously, I wasn't a part of Citracal's "target demo."

Though I did not take away the importance of maintaining bone density from the thousands of Paul Harvey or Citracal's messages I was exposed to, I did learn the power of appointment programming. Citracal, at that time a small concern in the world of supplements, managed to become a household name for a select segment of America without having to pepper the airwaves of TV and radio the way Budweiser and Ford did. Citracal wisely found a segment of their target customer base they could afford to reach, and then they communicated with those customers over and over again.

People are creatures of habit. They have listening, viewing, and reading patterns that strategic advertising can effectively reach. This understanding shaped the placement of every ad campaign of which I've been a part.

This is known as "bench mark" or "strip placement." Instead of a vertical frequency that involves chance and the hope that your campaign will reach the bulk of an audience, this tactical placement drives repetition to the same people over and over. That group might be fewer in number, but the likelihood of your message reaching the same people repeatedly is higher.

Most often, radio ad reps will suggest daytime audience plans (DAPs) which go in radio from 6 a.m. to 7 p.m., total audience plans (TAPs) that air from 6 a.m. to midnight or run of schedule plans (ROS), which air 24-7. DAP, TAP, and ROS schedules in radio can be rendered down even farther to day part – including morning drive, mid-day, and afternoon drive – and evenings.

The widely accepted standard in radio is that listeners need to be exposed to an emotion-evoking ad a minimum of seven times before they will react to that message. And listeners have to be in need of that product or service before they will react. Furthermore, the price needs to be right.

Let's say you, as an advertiser, are instructed by your ad rep to buy a 90-day DAP ad campaign. For simplicity's sake, let's assume your price is right. Let's say that the 30-second ads each cost $45 per play, and this schedule will have you receiving four ads a day for the 90-day campaign for a total investment of $16,200. Your 360 ads will now air for the next three months anywhere from 6 a.m. to 7 p.m. Radio audiences are measured by the average quarter hour, or AQH. In each of your 13-hour schedules, there are 52 quarter hours. The likelihood of your ad running at the same time every day is very small, as people are creatures of habit, so that results in the lapse of continuity. That leaves us with hope that the frequency of four ads in a single day will provided enough repetition to drive recall and generate a response. Use your own experience. When was the last time you listened to the radio for more than one hour? How about four hours? Or seven hours? So with this DAP schedule, your ad rep is asking you to rely on the frequency of four ads over the course of 13 hours.

Now, imagine how lucky you'd have to be to see results from a TAP package (6 a.m. to midnight) or an ROS package that could air anywhere around the clock. This is absurd.

When placing radio, TV, or cable ads, follow this rule of thumb. Always buy long-term contracts that are in the same spot break every day in the same program. Don't buy an ad in Letterman's Late Show; buy an ad every Monday through Friday for a year. Don't just buy a flight of ads on Memorial Day weekend on the History Channel, buy ads in every episode of Ice Road – Axmen, etc.,

Remember it's better to say the something 500 times to

500 people than it is to say something 5 times to 50,000. Never place an ad schedule shorter than 12 months, and if you can afford two benchmarked ads every hour of every day on every station in your marketplace, and it's the right thing for your business, buy it! If you can't afford the entire market, then purchase two benchmarked ads every day on a group of stations. If you can't afford a group of stations, then just purchase two ads a day on a single station. If you can't afford two benchmarked ads on a single station, then buy fewer hours. The minimum you want to do is a single bench-marked ad for one year on one station in the same exact commercial break.

In regard to print placement, find the section or sections in your paper or magazine that you feel the largest segment of your prospective customer base will read routinely and only advertise in that segment consistently for a minimum of one year.

When dealing with outdoor signage, secure the same space for a year, or don't waste your money.

In consideration of digital marketing solutions, please remember that we are really communicating with existing customers. We are improving our relationship with people who have already honored us with their business. These burgeoning forms of communication now allow us to have better contact and to recycle our present customers. I advocate that every business, regardless of your services or goods, engage in consistent email campaigns to your customers.

If you expect to see results with your email efforts, you'll need repetition. This is why it's advisable to send a coherent communication via email to your customers twice a month or once a week. Keep your email image-driven and with a single call to action. Most often, that call to action should be "click here," and then direct that email recipient to a landing page where they can redeem a coupon, fill out a form, or get more information about your products. Subject lines are key in realizing strong email open ratios. Keep it brief, ask questions, and, in order to avoid spam filters, avoid terms like "free" or "limited-time offer" and avoid the use of exclamation points. Most Web-based email platforms allow you to instantly integrate your email campaign with your business' Facebook page, Twitter page, LinkedIn profile, etc. Utilize that integration opportunity, so you have a coherent campaign on all of those forums.

When dealing with email marketing, Facebook fans, or Twitter followers, it's important that you actively recruit email addresses and new fans every day. If you operate a car dealership, then offer a raffle item for those who give you their email addresses when they test drive a car (be sure they know they're opting into your email blasts). If your business is a restaurant, then offer a frequent-diner deal that involves an incentive diners who serve up their email addresses.

The best businesses get creative and find a worthy local charity to be the benefactor of some promotion once that business has a certain amount of email addresses and a certain number of Facebook fans or Twitter followers.

Someone who knew a little something about communicating with followers once said, "Whatever words we utter should be chosen with care, for people will hear them and be influenced by them for good or ill." Buddha was wise, indeed.

CHAPTER 23
GOOD ADS CAN'T CHANGE A BAD BUSINESS

Several years ago, I had the pleasure of coaching a bright, young ad agency rep who handled the placement and creative of advertisements for TV, radio, print, and direct mail for a very large carpet store.

This store was a lumbering, stand-alone enterprise not affiliated with any franchise. It was independently owned by a gentleman who was third generation in this business.

When this rep with whom I was working got this big account, the carpet store had a vast selection of products and competitive prices. The rep, business owner, and I put together a strategic marketing plan, complete with a powerful jingle campaign for TV and radio; an aggressive, consistent, annual bench-marked placement; stellar copy; a new logo; signage to be installed; a website; and a promotional calendar. We couldn't miss.

The campaign started, and we all waited for results to manifest.

We began to track the campaign. One month into our efforts, the rep and I made an unannounced call on the business at their single location in a bustling part of town.

It was 10 a.m. when we stopped by, and the doors were locked. We could see people in the back of the store working, but they were too far away to see us. The sign at the entrance said "Open Monday - Saturday 9 a.m. - 8 p.m." We waited around for 10 minutes and then left.

We came back the next day, this time at 9:10 AM. This time we were met by a surly employee with no uniform who rudely unlocked the door and didn't acknowledge us as we walked in. The owner was nowhere to be found; we were told he was on vacation for the next week.

We then inquired about that month's promotional sale, and none of the employees knew anything about a sale. This was disheartening, because there were copious ads in that market that we spent hours writing, laying out, producing, placing, and scheduling. One of the employees said that a few customers had been by the day before asking about it, but he didn't know what they were talking about.

The next month, we asked the owner about falling away from the plan, and he became defensive claiming he did engage the sale.

Three months later, I was back in town, and we went to see the carpet store again. This time, the store was open, but I noticed the new signage we had ordered was still not installed. It was also hard not to notice the disarray in the entrance area of the store. Open boxes were all over the place, and it was obvious the place hadn't been cleaned in a while. In fact, at the receiving checkout area, there were the sticky remnants of an unidentified red drink spilled long ago. Who would really want to buy new "clean" carpet from this dirty place?

As usual, the owner wasn't in. Before we left, we requested that he call us.

Back at the agency, two hours later, we received our requested call. The carpet storeowner was irate because "the advertisements weren't working!" He wanted answers. I politely told the owner that we would consult the agency's principals and call him back. I then recommended to the agency and the young rep that they voluntarily resign the account. We called him back and, without emotion, fired the client.

Buddha once said, "No one saves us but ourselves. No one can and no one may. We ourselves must walk the path."

This business owner was expecting our good ads to change his bad business. This is impossible. The best advertisements in the world can't make him have his employees honor the promotional calendar that we installed, can't make him open his business on time, or change the attitude of a dismal staff that lacks the proper guidance to be great. So, we moved on. Eventually, the carpet store closed, and the young rep went on to handle and succeed with many major accounts.

No matter if you're a businessperson placing the ads, or a salesperson working to garner results on behalf of a client, it is a true partnership.

CHAPTER 24
COLLECTIONS AND
AVOIDING ATTRITION

Buddha once said "There are only two mistakes one can make along the road to truth; not going all the way, and not starting."

When selling or buying, we make a commitment to honor a truth. Many of us second-guess ourselves when it comes to honoring that truth, and sometimes "truth" is forsaken by "not going all the way." In the early part of my career, I, like many sellers, spent much of my time aiding in the delivery of products and then waiting to get paid for that service. Sometimes my clients paid, sometimes they paid late, sometimes they decided not to pay at all.

I would allow this, because I had a disproportionate sense of importance for my customer over myself and the enterprise that I represented. I needed the money owed just as desperately as the client that didn't pay (or more so), but the same amiable personality that allowed me to develop a relationship, build trust, and broker a sale, didn't want to disappoint them with the news that "you need to pay." So when it came to bearing the burden of disappointment, I usually ended up carrying that weight.

If a hard-won client who signed a contract – a client whom I had worked to please – wanted to back out of an agreement, quit early, or not honor certain terms of our agreement, I usually let them. After a couple years of realizing my budget goals but not seeing all that I should have on my paycheck, I decided to make a drastic shift in myself and investigate why these clients choose not to fulfill their end of the agreements that we both signed.

After much introspective meditation, I came to the realization that my time and energy was every bit as important as anyone else's. I knew that never had a time gone by when I intentionally didn't fulfill my end of an agreement. And if ever there was a failing, I did all that was in my power to make it right. I knew the clients who signed agreements with me expected me to carry out my end of our commitment, and so it was at that point I internally found validity in making my clients honor their ends of the agreements.

The unmistakable reality is that when you ask clients if they'd like to buy your products under the terms you're offering, they either give you a "yes" or "no," and they either sign or they don't. By signing this agreement to do business with you, you both have agreed to go all the way "down the road to truth," as Buddha put it.

In my time training, hiring, and coaching sellers of all ilk, I've found many struggle with the same woes I did early on in my sales career. If you have grappled internally with this, then ask yourself these questions:

1. Did I do everything promised when we agreed?

2. Does my product work?

3. Were the terms clear when the client signed the agreement?

If the answer was yes on all counts, then please remember that it is not you who are failing or attempting not to honor the agreement, it's the client, and what others do, think say is out of our control. Attempting to control outside forces only leads to internal suffering. The only thing we can command is our thoughts, words, and actions.

If your next course of action involves insisting they fulfill the agreement, then that's what you do – the results are out of your hands. Whether or not they decide to honor the agreement they signed is up to them. If they fail to honor the agreement, and your next action is to send them to collections, then that's the action you command. Whether they choose to pay the collections agent or not is their decision. If they don't pay the collections notices, and the next action is to summon them to court, then that's the action you command. Whether they choose to flee to Mexico or turn up to face the judge is their decision. Focus only on the actions you can command, and relinquish the results of those actions to the universe.

I mentioned I did some research as to why some of these clients chose not to fulfill their ends of bargains. I started by examining industries that realized no or low contract attrition and business models that had high volume of no-pay or late-pay clients who failed to honor the terms of the agreements they signed.

I found three different industries that had a relatively low contract attrition ratio:

1. The airline industry.

2. The hotel industry.

3. The wireless phone industry.

All three of these bustling fields shared points of commonality.

1. They enforced their contracts to the letter with all who

signed, no exceptions. If they did make an occasional exception, then they would likely not be doing the most honorable thing by all of the other customers who were fulfilling the terms of their agreements.

2. All offered a fleeting, intangible service. When someone orders specialty lumber from a lumber store, and it arrives, the likelihood of that customer bailing out on the bill would be slim, because it is a tangible commodity. We can touch the lumber and smell it, and it took infrastructure to get it here. With intangible products or services, people tend to hold them in less regard.

3. All had very clear terms of agreement. "You're purchasing a coach seat on Delta Airlines flying from San Francisco to Omaha on January 8 at 8:30 p.m. for $424."

4. All collected payment for services before services were engaged. The cell phone industry was the loosest on this, but they were stricter on falling behind and honoring the length of the agreement.

5. All required some credentials. You have to have an ID and at least a debit or credit card to get a hotel room.

The model I examined that had a high rate of people who didn't pay or fulfill the terms of their agreements was hospital emergency rooms.

For obvious reasons, many who utilize a hospital's emergency room rather than making an appointment with urgent care clinics do it because they lack insurance. Others, who are having a real emergency, put the priority of a payment on the back shelf. They are, after all, having a medical emergency. That low prioritization often results in a lack of payment.

Also, if the patient gets better as a result of that emergency room visit, some fail to justify why they would need to pay for something they no longer need. Though they, too, offered a fleeting product like the other industries, they failed to rigidly enforce their contracts with patients.

Unlike the other three industries that achieved low contract attrition, the hospital emergency room agreements were long, complicated, and seldom-read by those who signed. Different from the low attrition industries, hospitals required no credentials (thankfully, they help anyone in need) and payment is requested after the services have been rendered.

Unfortunately, many various industries foster the "emergency room" billing model. Most often, the reason people don't fulfill the obligation of that model is not because of malice or ill intent; it's because that model is conducive to failure.

Odds are, if you're selling in an environment like the emergency room billing model, you are likely the party initiating deals. If that is the case, then you're likely in a position to effect change in the way you bill, collect, and construct contracts. If that is the case, then consider implementing these changes:

1. Keep the contract verbiage succinct and simple. Many contract disputes arise because one party claims it was unclear about what was signed.

2. Only accept credit cards on a pre-flight basis. Allowing an auto-debit system to automatically bill your clients cards each month before they've received their services will make collections and

billing nightmares non-existent. Be sure the terms of the authorization are spelled out vividly on the agreement.

3. Offer a reasonable, short-rate, early-exit option for the client. Something like, "Buyer will pay 40 percent of the remaining value of the agreement should you terminate before the conclusion of this contract." That rate is enough of a "carrot or stick" incentive for them to fulfill the agreement to receive the remainder of their services.

4. Enforce your contracts if someone attempts to terminate sooner than agreed upon. You owe it to the other buyers who are honorably fulfilling their terms of agreement.

5. Require credentials. If you're dealing with an unsavory buyer who can't produce a credit card and a couple of vendor references, then you won't be doing either party a favor by engaging in a fruitless agreement that leads to drama.

If you're worried your clients will baulk when you attempt to implement this new billing protocol, just remember that people buy what is sold.

This was illustrated to me by St. Jude Children's Research Hospital in Memphis, Tenn. If you're not acquainted with this wonderful hospital, it is one of the leading pediatric cancer research facilities in the world. St. Jude openly shares its cancer treatment research freely with the world. Its primary source of funding is the donations it receives from everyday people. I'm convinced that one day cancer will be cured, and I believe it will be cured in Memphis at St. Jude Children's Research Hospital.

ZEN AND THE ART OF SALES

I first began fundraising for St. Jude in 1999 during a radio fundraiser. That year, St. Jude mailed us a blue print with suggestions about how we might best raise funds on the radio. Problem was, I failed to read it.

We got on the air, extolled the virtues of St. Jude, took phone calls and encouraged listeners to "give what ever they could." We said things like "every penny counts." We received donations ranging from $5 to $100 from thousands of listeners. By the end of the radiothon, we were please with our overall result, having helped amass thousands of dollars for this worthy cause and raised awareness about cancer research.

The next year, St. Jude sent a representative to help our station coordinate that year's fundraising efforts. She informed us that rather than asking people to "give what they could," we should ask people to become "partners in hope" with an ongoing donation automatically applied to their credit cards each month. We were skeptical about whether people would be willing to donate $240, as the year prior our largest , single donation was just $200. She also discouraged us from saying "every penny counts." In year two, we gave examples about what a single partner in hope's donation could accomplish. Like, "You could be paying for the test-tube that holds the very thing that helps save a child's life." The end result was a 300-percent increase in donations from the same market from the year prior. This new tactic allowed us to better help our listeners, help St. Jude, and help us all *make action happen faster*.

CHAPTER 25
YOUR JOURNEY

When my sales career began long ago, it was evident to me that I was meant to be in a role that involved helping others.

I found sales to be rewarding and became fast friends with many of my clients. Over time, as bars were raised and pressures increased, my life slowly changed to include stress, anxiety, fear, sleepless nights, epic highs, and debilitating lows. I pinned my happiness or misery on the actions of others.

I became obsessed with what just happened and what might happen next, whether it be either good or bad.

Sales, the thing that I had once enjoyed, was causing my severe suffering. To alleviate this suffering, I attempted to gain tighter control over my life. This only resulted in deeper suffering.

Sound familiar?

All people want the same thing. Everyone wants peace with fleeting pulses of joy. Even if they can't express that simple desire, that is why everyone does everything. Many people do many strange things with the hopes that their actions will result in their peace or joy.

I hope this modest book helps you find peace and joy on your journey.

Here's something that has helped me on my journey.

I've included Buddha's "Four Nobel Truths" and the "Eightfold Path." There are many interpretations and variations of both, so I've included my interpretation.

THE FOUR NOBLE TRUTHS

Suffering exists

Life is consists of growing old, getting sick, and dying. We all endure emotional suffering, including anxiety, fear, anger, loneliness, aggravation, pain, grief, despair, boredom, humiliation, and disappointment.

There is a cause for suffering

Suffering is caused by our craving to control things. That impulse can manifest in many shapes: the desire to evade unpleasant feelings, such as distress, disgust, fear, rage, and envy.

There is an end to suffering

Suffering can be vanquished; peace and joy can be achieved. True joy and serenity are attainable if we relinquish our desire to control. Suffering will subside if we learn to live each day at a time, not fixated on the past, future, or potential negative outcomes from today's actions. Present-moment awareness leads to peace and joy. Devoting less energy to past or future negative outcomes allows us more power to help others. This is Nirvana.

To end suffering, you must follow the Eightfold Path

The fourth truth is that the Eightfold Path is *the* path, the one that leads to the end of suffering. The Eightfold Path centers our focus on being aware of our actions, thoughts, and words. The path to enlightenment, or Nirvana, found by nurturing and striving for virtue, knowledge, and meditation.

THE EIGHTFOLD PATH

1. Right view
Grasp the meaning of Karma: People are the owners of their actions. Whatever actions they take, either positive or negative, belong to them.

2. Right intention
We should aspire to rid ourselves of qualities we know to be wrong and immoral. We can discern the differences between right intention and wrong intention.

3. Right speech
This includes abstaining from false speech, hurtful language, and idle chatter.

4. Right action
All actions ripen into events. The universe loves progress regarding everything. Be an agent of progress.

5. Right livelihood
Be as harmless as possible in your occupation. Contribute to the soul of your enterprise. Inspire confidence and security. Be considerate, generate abundance, and relieve suffering.

6. Right effort
Follow the path of least resistance. Life should be effortless. Apply effort to your actions, and detach from the results.

7. Right mindfulness
If you can't help someone, then at least don't hurt them. Avoid greed, anger, and ignorance. Foster generosity and understanding.

8. Right concentration
Find clarity by holding the mind and body still. Search for the ultimate truth via meditation. Meditation helps one to focus, find introspective peace, and increase creativity. Meditation reduces fear and anxiety.

Namaste,
Blake

BLAKE MESSER

Zen and the Art of Sales
An Eastern Approach to Western Commerce

ABOUT THE AUTHOR

Blake Messer is a Seattle-based advertising consultant. In recent years, he has been the keynote speaker for a 57-city international speaking tour that addressed over 19,000 entrepreneurs on methods they could utilize to more effectively communicate with existing and prospective customers.

These "Stronger Business" workshops were sponsored by over 60 of America's leading Chambers of Commerce.

His company has consulted more than 190 radio and television stations in markets large and small. Messer has hired, trained, and coached scores of sales people. In addition, he has steered more than 1,600 advertising campaigns on various media. His advertising efforts over the years have influenced untold millions and stimulated billions of dollars in commerce for hometown entrepreneurs and publicly traded companies.

For more information go to www.blakemesser.com, for a free guided meditation sales podcast, go to www.zenandtheartofsales.com.

Made in the USA
San Bernardino, CA
14 December 2016